My Ponderings

MICHAEL SCANTLEBURY

ISBN 978-1-4866-2157-6
eBook ISBN 978-1-4866-2158-3

Word Alive Press
119 De Baets Street Winnipeg, MB R2J 3R9
www.wordalivepress.ca

WORD ALIVE
—PRESS—

Cataloguing in Publication information is can be obtained from Library and Archives Canada.

CONTENTS

BOOKS BY MICHAEL SCANTLEBURY

Introduction

The Cambridge dictionary defines ponder, this way: to think carefully about something, especially for a noticeable length of time.

I believe that this is an art that has been lost in many circles. We need to take the time to think on things that are important long and deep. As a matter when reading the Scriptures, especially the Psalms we keep encountering the word *Selah*. That word *Selah* carries the following meaning in the original Hebrew:

- To pause and consider
- Stop and listen
- Extol or lift up
- To underline or highlight or reinforce: give emphasis to
- Amen or So be it
- To hand measure or weigh
- Think, contemplate, meditate

Anyone that comes to God MUST first believe that HE IS and then, that He is a rewarded to those who diligently seek Him. [Hebrews 11:6]

I do believe that this is our *ground zero* in pondering things pertaining to life. We must first get to the point of pure faith and believe that God exist and that He always did, is and forever will be. Because without this firm, faith-filled belief our pondering cannot truly begin.

Scripture informs us that this Eternal, Self-Existing God Who always was, is and forever will be; has given birth to everyone with a measure of faith, according to Romans 12:3 *For by the grace given to me, I tell everyone among you not to think of himself more highly than he should think.* Instead, think sensibly, as God has distributed a measure of faith to each one.

And I do believe that faith is exactly what we all need to begin our journey to deeply ponder the Creator of life!

Here is another important point. We just cannot get into 'God's Space' anytime we choose, no, we must be invited in. And as the Holy Scriptures tell us: that without faith it is IMPOSSIBLE to please God [Hebrews 11:6]. God decided from the very beginning of our existence to provide for us a measure of that faith. So now we have the means to enter. However, we would need to press the 'pause button' here as I love to ponder deeply, and this is not what this introduction is being written to accomplish. So, let us get into the meat if this book with some of my Ponderings on different topics. The chapters before you span my many years of pondering on several different subjects in the Lord. And as He has responded I have chronicled them and present to you in this book. It is my prayer and sincere hope that you would be both blessed and encouraged as you work through the pages of this book. Here we go, beginning with My Ponderings on the Kingdom of God.

CHAPTER ONE
MY PONDERINGS ON THE KINGDOM OF GOD

WHEN GOD CREATED MAN, HE NEVER INTENDED FOR MANKIND TO PRACTICE some kind of RELIGION; His heart was always KINGDOM! God's desire was for man to extend His Kingdom here on earth; so that's why when He created them, and He declared that they were to have Dominion!

So the plan of God was always to have a Kingdom here on earth and to have Citizens in this Kingdom. However, as we know citizenship is counted as a privilege to outsiders. It is reserved to those who are born in a country or is conferred upon those to whom the governing authority chooses. Hence the reason everyone needs to be Born Again to enter the Kingdom. Once we are Born Again, we are not born into a religion but into the Kingdom of God!

The Kingdom of God is not to be confused with Heaven. Heaven is God's Dwelling Place and the Kingdom of God comes out of Heaven. The Kingdom of God is sometimes referred to as "the Kingdom of Heaven" because that's where It originated from, as is revealed in the following passages: Matthew 5:3 states,

Blessed are the poor in spirit, For theirs is the kingdom of heaven.

Matthew 12:44-45

Again, the kingdom of heaven is like treasure hidden in a field, which a man found and hid; and for joy over it he goes and sells all that he has and buys that field. Again, the kingdom of heaven is like a merchant seeking beautiful pearls...

Matthew 25:1

Then the kingdom of heaven shall be likened to ten virgins who took their lamps and went out to meet the bridegroom.

2 Timothy 4:18

And the Lord will deliver me from every evil work and preserve me for His heavenly kingdom. To Him be glory forever and ever. Amen!

Some people perceive the Kingdom to be in Heaven and has no relationship to the world. So these people have no contact with the world. However, we need to understand this, the Kingdom is **not of this world but It works in the world**. The Kingdom of God is not Heaven; as the writer stated earlier, the Kingdom of God is also called the Kingdom of Heaven, signifying that It came from Heaven and is NOT Heaven Itself.

Some people believe that the Kingdom is the nation Israel. They see the Kingdom as purely earthly, seen as a political structure and when gathered together the Kingdom is released. These people are of the opinion that Jesus will come through the Eastern Gate of Israel, He will set up His headquarters in a building and all peoples will gather to Jerusalem. This view has a serious affect on eschatology. When we subscribe to this view we will want to be baptized in the Jordan River, touch the tomb that Jesus was buried in, etc.

We need to fully understand that the Kingdom was never promised exclusively to Israel.

- When Adam sinned, God always intended to bring restoration to mankind through His Son and everything He did was centred on this fact.

- To do this God raised up a man called Abraham and promised him that He would give him a son and that through him ALL THE NATIONS (not just one nation) of the earth would be blessed!
- We know that Abraham had a son named Isaac and the nation of Israel came (Isaac had two sons Jacob and Esau; God chose Jacob and later changed his name to Israel and from him came the twelve sons later known as the twelve tribes of Israel).
- The Israelites were reminded of this from generation to generation, that the Messiah King would come through them and the nations of the earth would be blessed.
- However, the Israelites as a people misunderstood the promise and made themselves the object of the promise rather than the conduit of it.
- Because of that misunderstanding, they developed a self-centred religion that condemned the world they were appointed to deliver the Redeemer to.
- God never intended for Israel to become a religion (Judaism) but rather "A Kingdom of Priests" unto Him.

Exodus 19:5-6

Now therefore, if you will indeed obey My voice and keep My covenant, then you shall be a special treasure to Me above all people; for all the earth is Mine. And you shall be to Me a kingdom of priests and a holy nation.' These are the words which you shall speak to the children of Israel.

Hence the reason the Jews wanted to know if Jesus was going to restore the Kingdom to Israel before He left earth as in shown in the following passage: Acts 1:1-8 says,

"Truly, O Theophilus, I made the first report as to all things that Jesus began both to do and teach until the day He was taken up, having given directions to the apostles whom He chose, through the Holy Spirit; to whom He also presented Himself living after His suffering by many infallible proofs, being seen by them through forty days, and speaking of the things pertaining to the kingdom of

God. And having met with them, He commanded them not to depart from Jerusalem, but to await the promise of the Father which you heard from Me. For John truly baptized with water, but you shall be baptized in the Holy Spirit not many days from now. Then, indeed, these coming together, they asked Him, saying, Lord, do You at this time restore the kingdom to Israel? And He said to them, It is not for you to know the times or the seasons, which the Father has put in His own authority. But you shall receive power, the Holy Spirit coming upon you. And you shall be witnesses to Me both in Jerusalem and in all Judea, and in Samaria, and to the end of the earth." [removing their mindset from a purely Jewish perspective to that of a Global one] MKJV [Parenthesis added]!

Please understand this—from the fall of man, everything was centred on the coming of Messiah King; all the prophecies were about His arrival and what He would bring.

Here are some Scriptures used in this misconception: John 18:36 says,

Jesus answered, "My kingdom is not of this world [cosmos or system]. If My kingdom were of this world, then My servants would fight so that I might not be delivered to the Jews. But now My kingdom is not from here." [Parenthesis added]

There are several Greek words that are translated into the English word "world"—however, the word used here for world is the Greek, cosmos—which is rendered system or arrangement. Or from where we get our English word "cosmetic"—superficial, makeup, ornamental, or aesthetic...

So the Jews needed to get the message that the Kingdom of God was not of this world's system: Luke 17:20-21 says,

And being asked by the Pharisees when the kingdom of God would come, He answered and said, "The kingdom of God does not come with observation. Nor shall they say, Lo here! or, behold, there! For behold, the kingdom of God is in your midst."

"Would come"—the question was asked with a strong Jewish mentality. Whenever they heard Kingdom they thought that Jesus would sit on the throne, they will overthrow the oppressors and rule.

The Kingdom is within you (KJV)—They were asking when would the Kingdom come—Jesus was saying that the Kingdom had already come. They removed the urgency and relevance of the Kingdom and refer all things to the future. Jesus constantly removes the futuristic nature.

Many believe that the Kingdom will come when Christians will get into politics and take over the government. In the medieval times the Pope really thought that the Kingdom was being exercised by dominating in the government. That false concept of dominion in no way liberated the Church. We do have the responsibility to get into politics but it can only be done by those who are graced to do it. Romans 14:17 says,

For the kingdom of God is not eating and drinking, but righteousness and peace and joy in the Holy Spirit.

The Kingdom is not fleshly and physically satisfying. The Kingdom is a deep internal work of the Spirit of God that propels man to a place of perfection. It is the work of the Spirit in the heart of man. The Kingdom is a deliberate drawing down of spiritual values into the inner man. It does not come by observation. The Kingdom is the uncontested rule and Government of God that is established first in the heart of man them moves outwardly to all humans.

Relationship says—"I cannot achieve a mandate that exceeds me, its fulfillment requires the pooling of intelligence and resources causing the creation of a corporate mind. From that perspective no relationship can be considered mundane and casual, intended for the tickling of one's emotion and to break personal loneliness. But relationship must be perceived as a primary currency of the Kingdom!"

Now remember that we are Ambassadors of the Kingdom of God and not the Church: If we are to busy ourselves promoting the Kingdom and seeking to advance His Kingdom in the earth then folks would not get bored with Church; instead it will become an exciting place to be as we are trained to Reign in this life as Kings! Oh that's awesome!

Allow me to present you with 17 truths about the Kingdom. There maybe more, I am sure:

1.   **The Kingdom was/is a Present Reality**—NOW—for us today. This can be noted with many of the Parables of The Kingdom that Jesus spoke about beginning with this phrase "The Kingdom of God IS..."

2.   **The Kingdom is NOT Fleshly**; that is, it is not based upon natural senses. We in this Kingdom are not moved by what we see or hear in the natural realm of

circumstances—John 18:36 *Jesus answered, "My kingdom does not belong to this world. If my kingdom belonged to this world, my servants would fight to keep me from being handed over to the Jews. But for now my kingdom is not from here."*

3.   **The Kingdom does/did Not Come With Observation**—Luke 17:20 *And being asked by the Pharisees when the kingdom of God would come, He answered and said, "The kingdom of God does not come with observation."*

Observation—"In such a manner that it can be watched with the eyes; in a visible manner"; to take notice or cognizance of by the intellect...

4.   **The Kingdom is entered by the New Birth**—that is being Born Again of Water and of The Spirit (John 3:3). This experience gives us a new nature; even His Divine Nature. Remember that you have not been baptised into a religion but into the Kingdom of God!
Let's look at Colossians 1:13 and 1 Peter 1:17-25

He has delivered us from the power of darkness and conveyed us into the kingdom of the Son of His love...

And if you call on the Father, who without partiality judges according to each one's work, conduct yourselves throughout the time of your stay here in fear; knowing that you were not redeemed with corruptible things, like silver or gold, from your aimless conduct received by tradition from your fathers, but with the precious blood of Christ, as of a lamb without blemish and without spot. He indeed was foreordained before the foundation of the world, but was manifest in these last times for you who through Him believe in God, who raised Him from the dead and gave Him glory, so that your faith and hope are in God. Since you have purified your souls in obeying the truth through the Spirit in sincere love of the brethren, love one another fervently with a pure heart, having been born again, not of corruptible seed but incorruptible, through the word of God which lives and abides forever, because "All flesh is as grass, And all the glory of man as the flower of the grass. The grass withers, And its flower falls away, But the word of the Lord endures forever." Now this is the word which by the gospel was preached to you.

5. **The Kingdom was/is at Hand**—that is, it is within your reach—Mark 1:14-15 *And after John was delivered up, Jesus came into Galilee, proclaiming the gospel of the kingdom of God, and saying, The time is fulfilled, and the kingdom of God draws near. Repent, and believe the gospel.*

God is extending His Kingdom to men everywhere today—the invitation is still open!

6. **The Kingdom took/takes Priority**—It comes First—Matthew 6:33 *But seek first the kingdom of God and His righteousness, and all these things shall be added to you.*
7. **The Kingdom was/is a Gift**; that is: It is ministered
8. to us abundantly through the Love, Mercy, and Grace of God.—Luke 12:31-32 *But rather seek the kingdom of God, and all these things shall be added to you. Do not fear, little flock, for it is your Father's good pleasure to give you the kingdom.*
2 Peter 1:1-11

Simon Peter, a servant and an apostle of Jesus Christ, to those who have obtained like precious faith with us through the righteousness of our God and our Saviour Jesus Christ, Grace and peace be multiplied to you through the knowledge of God and of Jesus our Lord, according as His divine power has given to us all things that pertain to life and godliness, through the knowledge of Him who has called us to glory and virtue, through which He has given to us exceedingly great and precious promises, so that by these you might be partakers of the divine nature, having escaped the corruption that is in the world through lust. But also in this very thing, bringing in all diligence, filling out your faith with virtue, and with virtue, knowledge; and with knowledge self-control, and with self-control, patience, and with patience, godliness, and with godliness, brotherly kindness, and with brotherly kindness, love. For if these things are in you and abound, they make you to be neither idle nor unfruitful in the knowledge of our Lord Jesus Christ. For he in whom these things are not present is blind and cannot see afar off and has forgotten that he was purged from his sins in the past. Therefore, brothers, rather be diligent to make your calling and election sure, for if you do these things, you shall never fall. For so an entrance shall be ministered to you abundantly into the everlasting kingdom of our Lord and Saviour Jesus Christ.

The Kingdom is marked by Violence (Not physical violence, but a mentality that nothing will stop you from fully entering into it)—Matthew 11:12 and Luke 16:16 says,

And from the days of John the Baptist until now the kingdom of Heaven is taken by violence and the violent take it by force.

The Law and the Prophets were until John. Since that time the kingdom of God is proclaimed, and everyone is pressing into it.

In essence we must conquer all obstacles, mindsets and hindrances with a Violent faith and confession!

9. **The Kingdom Demands Perseverance**—Luke 9:62 *And Jesus said to him, "No one, having put his hand to the plough and looking back, is fit for the kingdom of God."*
10. **The Kingdom is Marked by Power**—1 Corinthians 4:20 *For the kingdom of God is not in word, but in power.*—The word for power is the Greek word dunamis and refers to the might, ability, and strength of the Lord!
11. **The Kingdom is Supernatural**; that is, it goes above and beyond the realm of the natural—the strength and wisdom of man—

the ability and intellect of man. This gospel of the Kingdom is a Supernatural Gospel being ministered by Supernatural People. Mark 16:15-20 says,

And He said to them, "Go into all the world and preach the gospel to every creature. He who believes and is baptized will be saved; but he who does not believe will be condemned. And these signs will follow those who believe: In My name they will cast out demons; they will speak with new tongues; they will take up serpents; and if they drink anything deadly, it will by no means hurt them; they will lay hands on the sick, and they will recover." So then, after the Lord had spoken to them, He was received up into heaven, and sat down at the right hand of God. And they went out and preached everywhere, the Lord working with them and confirming the word through the accompanying signs. Amen.

12. **The Kingdom involves Persecution and Tribulation and Affliction**—Acts 14:22—*confirming the souls of the disciples, calling on them to continue in the faith and that through much tribulation we must enter into the kingdom of God.*

Again we can see that the half-hearted will not fight the good fight of faith. This walk is for overcomers who are victorious in Jesus Christ!

13. **The Kingdom is Stable and Cannot Be Moved**—Hebrews 12:26-29

whose voice then shook the earth; but now He has promised, saying, "Yet once more I will not only shake the earth, but also the heavens." And this word, "Yet once more," signifies the removing of those things that are shaken, as of things that have been made, so that the things which cannot be shaken may remain. Therefore, since we are receiving a kingdom that cannot be shaken, let us have grace, by which we may serve God acceptably with reverence and godly fear, for also, "Our God is a consuming fire."
Everything else BUT the Kingdom of God is currently in a state of Shaking and Falling!

14. **The Kingdom is an Everlasting Kingdom**—1 Peter 1:11 and Luke 1:31-33 says,

For so an entrance shall be ministered to you abundantly into the everlasting kingdom of our Lord and Saviour Jesus Christ.

And behold! You shall conceive in your womb and bear a son, and you shall call His name JESUS. He shall be great and shall be called the Son of the Highest. And the Lord God shall give Him the throne of His father David. And He shall reign over the house of Jacob forever, and of His kingdom there shall be no end.

15. **The Kingdom was/is to be Taken to the Whole Earth**—Please understand that the earth has heard "a" gospel But not "This" Gospel of the Kingdom!

Is there another gospel? Well the Apostle Paul says so in 2 Corinthians 11:3-4 and Galatians 1:6-12 let's read these two passages from the KJV; as a matter of fact the Apostle Paul pronounced a curse on anyone who preaches another gospel—strong words! Here is what they say,

But I fear, lest by any means, as the serpent beguiled Eve through his subtilty, so your minds should be corrupted from the simplicity that is in Christ. For if he that cometh preacheth another Jesus, whom we have not preached, or if ye receive another spirit, which ye have not received, or another gospel, which ye have not accepted, ye might well bear with him.

I marvel that ye are so soon removed from him that called you into the grace of Christ unto another gospel: Which is not another; but there be some that trouble you, and would pervert the gospel of Christ. But though we, or an angel from heaven, preach any other gospel unto you than that which we have preached unto you, let him be accursed. As we said before, so say I now again, if any man preach any other gospel unto you than that ye have received, let him be accursed. For do I now persuade men, or God? Or do I seek to please men? For if I yet pleased men, I should not be the servant of Christ. But I certify you, brethren, that the gospel which was preached of me is not after man. For I neither received it of man, neither was I taught it, but by the revelation of Jesus Christ.

16. **The Kingdom Is Within You**—Luke 17:20-21 KJV

And when he was demanded of the Pharisees, when the kingdom of God should come, he answered them and said, The kingdom of God cometh not with observation: Neither shall they say, Lo here! or, lo there! for, behold, the kingdom of God is within you.

"Within you"—How does that translate? Colossians 1:25-29 KJV says,

of which I became a minister, according to the administration of God given to me for you, to fulfill the Word of God; the mystery which has been hidden from ages and from generations, but now has been revealed to His saints. For to them God would make known what are the riches of the glory of this mystery among the nations, which is Christ [The Anointed One] in you, the hope of glory, whom we preach, warning every man and teaching every man in all wisdom, so that we may present every man perfect in Christ Jesus. For which I also labour, striving according to the working of Him who works in me in power. [Parenthesis added]

That word or designation for Jesus speaks of "The Anointed One" so there is An Anointed One IN you.

Now hear this, there were three kinds of people Anointed in the Scriptures:

- Prophets (1 Kings 19:16 *Also you shall anoint Jehu the son of Nimshi as king over Israel. And Elisha the son of Shaphat of Abel Meholah you shall anoint as prophet in your place.*)—To declare God unto man!
- Priests (Exodus 40:13-15 *You shall put the holy garments on Aaron, and anoint him and consecrate him, that he may minister to Me as priest. And you shall bring his sons and clothe them with tunics. You shall anoint them, as you anointed their father, that they may minister to Me as priests; for their anointing shall surely be an everlasting*

priesthood throughout their generations.)—To bring men unto God!
- •Kings (1 Samuel 16:13 *Then Samuel took the horn of oil and anointed him in the midst of his brothers; and the Spirit of the Lord came upon David from that day forward. So Samuel arose and went to Ramah.*)— To rule with authority!

17. The Kingdom of God is in the Holy Ghost and is marked by Righteousness, Peace and Joy—Romans 14:17 *for the kingdom of God is not eating and drinking, but righteousness and peace and joy in the Holy Spirit.*

So in essence when we received the Holy Ghost He brought the Kingdom; which is Righteousness, Peace and Joy IN the Holy Ghost.

The Kingdom is not intended to stay in us; it starts in our hearts and goes out. It is not just nice principles we collect in our hearts—this cannot just be information—it must adjust our lives.

There is a dimension of the Kingdom that encompasses the whole world. The Kingdom is everywhere where God is (every political, sporting, economic, etc.). We must remove the idea that the Kingdom is just a religious structure.

Beware of A Passive Mind—God does not allow His Kingdom to advance through passivity—the Kingdom of God suffers violence and forceful men advance it... The devil loves passive Christians—remember that it is the righteous who are as bold as a lion—get your roar on and advance the Kingdom!

We need to remember that there are two kingdoms operating in the world: the Kingdom of God and the kingdom of satan or darkness! In light of this, I would like to re-visit king Nebuchadnezzar's dream and its interpretation as it reveals some very pertinent information concerning these two kingdoms and the eventual outcome. [I have written extensively on this in my book— "Daniel In Babylon" ordering details at the end of this book.]

Daniel is considered as one the most accurate of all end-time Prophets, and while he and his fellow Israelites were captive in Babylon, the God of Heaven caused King Nebuchadnezzar to have a dream, which he could not remember, let alone have it interpreted. The Lord then revealed both the dream and its interpretation to Daniel and it pertained to the kingdoms of this world and the debilitating effect/influence by the Kingdom of God on them! Let's read the following account: Daniel 2:31-47 says,

"You, O king, were looking and behold, there was a single great statue; that statue, which was large and of extraordinary splendour, was standing in front of you, and its appearance was awesome. "The head of that statue was made of fine gold, its breast and its arms of silver, its belly and its thighs of bronze, its legs of iron, its feet partly of iron and partly of clay. "You continued looking until a stone was cut out without hands, and it struck the statue on its feet of iron and clay and crushed them. "Then the iron, the clay, the bronze, the silver and the gold were crushed all at the same time and became like chaff from the summer threshing floors; and the wind carried them away so that not a trace of them was found. But the stone that struck the statue became a great mountain and filled the whole earth. The Interpretation -- Babylon the First Kingdom "This was the dream; now we will tell its interpretation before the king. "You, O king, are the king of kings, to whom the God of heaven has given the kingdom, the power, the strength and the glory; and wherever the sons of men dwell, or the beasts of the field, or the birds of the sky, He has given them into your hand and has caused you to rule over them all. You are the head of gold. Medo-Persia and Greece "After you there will arise another kingdom inferior to you, then another third kingdom of bronze, which will rule over all the earth. Rome "Then there will be a fourth kingdom as strong as iron; inasmuch as iron crushes and shatters all things, so, like iron that breaks in pieces, it will crush and break all these in pieces. "In that you saw the feet and toes, partly of potter's clay and partly of iron, it will be a divided kingdom; but it will have in it the toughness of iron, inasmuch as you saw the iron mixed with common clay. "As the toes of the feet were partly of iron and partly of pottery, so some of the kingdom will be strong and part of it will be brittle. "And in that you saw the iron mixed with common clay, they will combine with one another in the seed of men; but they will not adhere to one another, even as iron does not combine with pottery. The Divine Kingdom "In the days of those kings the God of heaven will set up a kingdom which will never be destroyed, and that kingdom will not

be left for another people; it will crush and put an end to all these kingdoms, but it will itself endure forever. "Inasmuch as you saw that a stone was cut out of the mountain without hands and that it crushed the iron, the bronze, the clay, the silver and the gold, the great God has made known to the king what will take place in the future; so the dream is true and its interpretation is trustworthy." Daniel Promoted Then King Nebuchadnezzar fell on his face and did homage to Daniel, and gave orders to present to him an offering and fragrant incense. The king answered Daniel and said, "Surely your God is a God of gods and a Lord of kings and a revealer of mysteries, since you have been able to reveal this mystery." NASU

In Daniel's interpretation of the dream, he was declaring and revealing the colliding of world systems. He was revealing the intent of God's Kingdom for coming into the earth! There are a few things that I would like to highlight from Daniel's interpretation.

In King Nebuchadnezzar's dream he saw a "*single great statue*".

The Hebrew word used to describe *great* here is the word *saggiy* and is rendered large in size and number but not great in terms of quality. In essence it is large and appears to be powerful, but it has no substance—this is what the Kingdom of God will confront.

This is what the kingdoms of this world [cosmos—worldly systems] are really like. Also note that in Nebuchadnezzar's dream the quality of this image is constantly diminishing in value. To the natural eye, the systems of this world may appear magnificent and astonishing at times but in reality, they diminish in value and quality.

In contrast the Kingdom of God, [the stone cut out of the mountain] described in king Nebuchadnezzar's dream, "*became a Great Mountain!*" The Hebrew word used for *great* is the word *rab*; and is described as—superior in rank, internal capacity, and describes leadership—to stand at the top. Daniel spent time explaining the grandeur of the statue and then compares it to a mountain. God pays attention to substance on the inside and not external appeal. Someone looking at these two images [i.e. the statute and the mountain] in the natural without any divine revelation would easily choose the statue, as its external appeal was much greater.

Daniel continued in his interpretation of the king's dream: *"You continued looking until a stone was cut out without hands, and it struck the statue on its feet of iron and clay and crushed them."* There was an impacting blow to the statue with no apparent source. The Kingdom of God is on a collision course with every system that bears the image of the statue. Every place this image is found it will be confronted!

The Kingdom like leaven starts out small but continues until the King of the Kingdom rules. The Kingdom of God is highly confrontational. The Kingdom of God has the power to completely transform. The rock [representing the Kingdom of God] spoken of in the Book of Daniel [Daniel 2:31-47] struck and all entities [gold, silver, bronze, iron and clay] and they crumbled at the same time! The Kingdom of God will always prove itself to be superior to all world systems. That is the Greatness of the Kingdom of God!!!

This stone [representing the Kingdom of God] grew and grew until it *"filled the whole earth"*—not just certain structures in the earth—all the earth!

I love when insecure men seek to close doors to you to advance the Kingdom of God, and the Holy Spirit without their help still open the doors for you without asking their permission!

As we close this chapter permit me to say this: The Kingdom and the Church are not one and the same! The Church is the Eccelesia or Senate of the Kingdom. It is a created entity, while the Kingdom of God always existed, just as God always existed... This brings us to the next chapter—My Ponderings on The Church!

Chapter Two
My Ponderings On The Church

For those of you who don't know it already, the Church is not an ornate building that houses preaching and a song service, but rather the Body of Believers in the Lord Jesus Christ! The Church that Jesus Christ is building is not being built with natural material but with the lives of people. Another fact that we need to grasp and understand is the fact that the Church that He is building is apostolic.

Jesus Christ the Builder of the Church is the Apostle who was the Sent One [Greek—apostello]—Hebrews 3:1 says,

> *Therefore, holy brethren, partakers of the heavenly calling, consider the Apostle and High Priest of our confession, Christ Jesus…*

If a carpenter was to build a house, he would build a wooden house. If a brick layer or mason was to build a house, he would build a concrete or brick house. In like manner Jesus Christ, The Apostle, is the One who is building the Church and as such the Church that He is building is apostolic.

The Church is not a building that is ornately decorated with gold, jewels or stained glass for that matter. The Church is not a building at all, but rather, the assembly of Believers, all to be discussed in a later chapter.

When Jesus Christ first used the word *Church* in Matthew Chapter 16 it was to introduce a whole new dynamic to His early Apostles. That word

Church comes from the Greek *ecclesia* meaning assembly. As a matter of fact, the Roman

Senate was also an ecclesia or assembly.

Eccelesia—which, means assembly, called-out-ones, conger-gation, a body of citizens gathered together to discuss the affairs of state [or any definite purpose].

Vines Dictionary:

Eccelesia—a calling out, meeting, congregation, community of members, assembly or church, from the roots meaning out and bid or call forth—Strong's Concordance.

Thayer's Lexicon says it this way:

Eccelesia—a gathering of citizens called out from their homes into some public place; an assembly; from the roots meaning 'out of [a place; a group, number, company, community, a state or condition]; a connection with a thing or person; a race, lineage, nativity, a governing power, etc... and to call aloud, utter in a loud voice, "to call forth from and into", to cause to pass from one state to another, to invite, to rouse or summon.

Just as Caesar had his Senate [his assembly of called-out-ones] Jesus Christ was declaring that He was going to have His Church [His Assembly of called-out-ones] to establish His Rule on earth.

The True Church will be the possessor of the Keys of the Kingdom of God. Ergo, accurate access to the Kingdom of God is through His Church. The Church must be built upon the revelation that comes from the Father and not through flesh and blood, i.e. traditions, festivals, holy days, works, etc!

The True Church has been given the power to bind and loose things in Heaven and on earth. The expressions *bind and loose* were common to Jewish legal phraseology meaning to declare something forbidden or to declare it allowed. Binding in the Greek is *deo* and it means to prohibit or forbid! Loose in the Greek is from the word *luo* and it means to wreck, release, unbind, set free or to undo!

Every building has a structural plan and the Church of Jesus Christ is no different. The Word of God is the blueprint for the foundational structure of the Church: Ephesians 2:20-21, which says,

> *built on the foundation of the apostles and prophets, with Christ Jesus himself as the chief cornerstone. In him the whole building is joined together and rises to become a holy temple in the Lord.*

The Church is built on the foundation of the Apostles and Prophets, with Jesus Christ as the Chief or Head Cornerstone!

Remember the Church that Jesus Christ is building is being built on Him and the doctrine that He releases by His Holy Spirit, to Apostles and Prophets who in turn release it to the Teachers and Ministers in the Church. This was firmly established when the Church began in the Book of Acts: Acts 2:36-44, which says,

> *"Therefore let all Israel be assured of this: God has made this Jesus, whom you crucified, both Lord and Christ." When the people heard this, they were cut to the heart and said to Peter and the other apostles, "Brothers, what shall we do?" Peter replied, "Repent and be baptized, every one of you, in the name of Jesus Christ for the forgiveness of your sins. And you will receive the gift of the Holy Spirit. The promise is for you and your children and for all who are far off-for all whom the Lord our God will call." With many other words he warned them; and he pleaded with them, "Save yourselves from this corrupt generation." Those who accepted his message were baptized, and about three thousand were added to their number that day. They devoted themselves to the apostles' teaching and to the fellowship, to the breaking of bread and to prayer. Everyone was filled with awe, and many wonders and miraculous signs were done by the apostles.*

When the Holy Spirit arrived on the Day of Pentecost and launched the Church, Apostle Peter was the first one used to preach Jesus Christ in order to ensure the authenticity of the revelation released to these early Believers. Of note is the fact the moment the people received the Word that Peter spoke, they were convicted and immediately entered into to the true Spirit of the Church and that of the early Apostles, when they addressed the Apostles as "Brothers" [verse 37]! This to me is very interesting as this was the very inception of the Church and the Twelve Apostles were referred to as Brothers by those now being saved. They immediately understood the fact that Apostle is more of a function than that of a title! They knew that there was an Apostolic Grace on Peter and the other Apostles so they immediately submitted to them and sought advice and direction.

The outcome of this momentous occasion was that they were water baptized and they continued steadfastly in the Apostles' doctrine and fellowship!

The Apostles' doctrine was and still is the key to the proper construction and function of the Church of Jesus Christ. As such it was vital that this "Apostles' doctrine" i.e. the preaching and teaching of Jesus Christ be successfully and securely passed on from generation to generation.

The Apostle Paul had to go through a major time of purging before he could be mightily used of the Lord in assisting to build His Church. In his life pre-Christ, he was Saul, a zealous Jew and according to the Jewish law, he was blameless! Philippians 3:4-9 says,

"though I also might have confidence in the flesh. If anyone else thinks he may have confidence in the flesh, I more so: circumcised the eighth day, of the stock of Israel, of the tribe of Benjamin, a Hebrew of the Hebrews; concerning the law, a Pharisee; concerning zeal, persecuting the church; concerning the righteousness which is in the law, blameless. But what things were gain to me, these I have counted loss for Christ. Yet indeed I also count all things loss for the excellence of the knowledge of Christ Jesus my Lord, for whom I have suffered the loss of all things, and count them as rubbish, that I may gain Christ and be found in Him, not having my own righteousness, which is from the law, but that which is through faith in Christ, the righteousness which is from God by faith."

The Lord had to strike him down to "detoxify" him from his religious ways. While on the road to Damascus, Paul's mission to persecute the early Church was cut short as the Lord struck him blind. He had to be emptied of his present beliefs and to be now filled with the true Doctrine of Jesus Christ in order to be used mightily to build the Church of Jesus Christ. The Lord went through great lengths in ensuring that the authentic Gospel got to His Church and He continues to do this. Ephesians 1:22-23 says,

> *And God placed all things under his feet and appointed him to be head over everything for the church, which is his body, the fullness of him who fills everything in every way.*

THE BODY OF JESUS CHRIST

First off let me say this—we relate to the world we live in through our bodies. It is in a body that we get things done in the world of time and space. That's why when God wanted to redeem the world back to Himself; He gave Jesus Christ a Body to come to earth in order to function. Similarly Jesus Christ relates to the world through us—His Body [the Church].

So as the Body of Jesus Christ in the earth, every Born-again Believer has a part in the Body. The Bible goes on to reveal that the Head of the Body is indeed Jesus Christ—both of the Universal Church and the local church. It also goes on to make a powerful statement when it says "*the Head cannot say to the feet, I have no need of you*" [1 Corinthians 12:21]. So when the Believer is feeling that they are of little consequence to the functioning of the Church, this passage assures us that it does not matter where or what place one has in the Body, that we are all needed!

The Bible goes on to give us at least seven different aspects of the Church. And just like our bodies having many parts but all making up this one body, in like manner the Church, the Body of Christ has many parts, all making up His Body.

Ephesians 2:10 reveals that the Church is God's Workmanship or Masterpiece according to the ISV translation!

> *For we are God's workmanship, created in Christ Jesus to do good works, which God prepared in advance for us to do.*
>
> *For we are his masterpiece, created in Christ Jesus for good works that God prepared long ago to be our way of life.* ISV

THE CHURCH AS GOD'S WORKMANSHIP/MASTERPIECE

The Greek word poiema that is translated into our English word workmanship does not really bring out the real significance of the word. However, poiema comes from the Latin poema, from which we get the English word *Poem*! So, in essence this word for workmanship is taken from a word that is descriptive of the arts and creativity so we could then translate Ephesians 2:10 to say that—"We are God's creative Masterpiece…"

Truly this is a humbling thought that the Creator of the universe and all that is in it would choose people like you and me to make up *His Creative Masterpiece*… The concept of a masterpiece lends to the idea that there must be other pieces in the puzzle. As such we can conclude that when the Church is placed alongside everything that God has created—the Church stands out far and above everything else! Ephesians 2:18-19 says,

> *It is through Christ that all of us, Jews and Gentiles, are able to come in the one Spirit into the presence of the Father. So then, you Gentiles are not foreigners or strangers any longer; you are now citizens together with God's people and members of the family of God.* GNB

As we explore the entirety of the New Testament; God's people are very seldom referred to by the title Christians or even Believers. The first recorded use of the term "Christian" is found in the New Testament, in Acts 11:26, which states *"…in Antioch the disciples were first called Christians."* The second mention of the term follows in Acts 26:28, where Herod Agrippa II replies to Paul the Apostle, *"Do you think that in such a short time you can persuade me to be a Christian?"* The third and final New Testament reference to the term is in 1 Peter 4:16, which exhorts Believers, *"…if you suffer as a Christian, do not be ashamed, but praise God that you bear that name."* [Wikipedia]

However, the most common collective title used for Christians is "brothers" which emphasizes the fact that we are members in one spiritual family. Remember that we have become members of God's Family [Household] because of Christ's sacrifice which gained us access because of His relationship to the Father! God's Family is determined by relationship to the Father...

In Greek the word used for family is patria and is derived from the word that is used for father—pater. Apostle Paul puts it beautifully in the following reference: Ephesians 3:14-15, which says,

> *For this reason I bow my knees to the Father of our Lord Jesus Christ, from whom the whole family in heaven and earth is named.*

There is a direct play on words "Father and Family"—showing that family comes from fatherhood. This is further clarified in: Hebrews 2:10-12, which says,

> *For it was fitting for Him, for whom are all things and by whom are all things, in bringing many sons to glory, to make the captain of their salvation perfect through sufferings. For both He who sanctifies and those who are being sanctified are all of one, for which reason He is not ashamed to call them brethren, saying: "I will declare Your name to My brethren; In the midst of the assembly I will sing praise to You."*

There is a simple yet powerful revelation contained in this passage: God has made us His sons through Jesus, and Jesus Himself is the Only Begotten Son, of God the Father. Because of this fact, Jesus acknowledges us as His brothers—because of our relationship to the Father. Remember that Jesus never did anything without His Father's leading and direction; and as such Jesus never called us "brothers" until He heard His Father calls us "sons". Once His Father referred to us as His sons, then Jesus acknowledged us as His brothers.

The local Christian church then, is to be a close-knit family of brothers and sisters. Brotherliness also provided a key guiding principle for the management of relationships between Christians; for example, we can read the following: Romans 4:15, 21, which says,

> *Yet if your brother is grieved because of your food, you are no longer walking in love. Do not destroy with your food the one for whom Christ died.... It is good neither to eat meat nor drink wine*

nor do anything by which your brother stumbles or is offended or is made weak.

1 Corinthians 6:8

No, you yourselves do wrong and cheat, and you do these things to your brethren!

1 Corinthians 8:11-13

And because of your knowledge shall the weak brother perish, for whom Christ died? But when you thus sin against the brethren, and wound their weak conscience, you sin against Christ. Therefore, if food makes my brother stumble, I will never again eat meat, lest I make my brother stumble.

2 Thessalonians 3:14-15

And if anyone does not obey our word in this epistle, note that person and do not keep company with him, that he may be ashamed. Yet do not count him as an enemy, but admonish him as a brother.

Philemon 15-16

For perhaps he departed for a while for this purpose, that you might receive him forever, no longer as a slave but more than a slave—a beloved brother, especially to me but how much more to you, both in the flesh and in the Lord.

James 4:11

Do not speak evil of one another, brethren. He who speaks evil of a brother and judges his brother, speaks evil of the law and judges the law. But if you judge the law, you are not a doer of the law but a judge.

Jesus insisted that His followers were true brothers and sisters and that none among them should act like the rabbis of His day who elevated themselves above their fellow countrymen: Ephesians 2:20-22, which says,

> *built on the foundation of the apostles and prophets, with Christ Jesus himself as the chief cornerstone. In him the whole building is joined together and rises to become a holy temple in the Lord. And in him you too are being built together to become a dwelling place in which God lives by his Spirit.*

In Hebrew the word for house is *beit* and carries the concept of a home or family. As a matter of fact, it is directly connected to the Hebrew word that translates "to build"! So, in Hebrew thinking there is a close connection between family and building. The word they used to translate "house" was not used to describe a dwelling place but rather a family or people. As a matter of fact we can notice the emphasis on building in the passage—*built, building, temple, built, dwelling place...* Five times, the thought is brought out here.

Most Believers know this, but I will still say it—no matter how beautiful the edifice is we build even with the best of natural materials, it is not the final Dwelling Place for the Lord! The truth is that His Temple is to be constructed with People! It is not being constructed with the most valuable materials on the planet like diamonds, gold, silver or marble but with *people*!!!

Every Believer has the privilege of providing his/her own physical body to the Holy Spirit as a temple to dwell in. God has redeemed our bodies so that it might be a temple for His Spirit!!! Once again we are warned to be careful that we do not defile or destroy the temple—whether the Collective or Individual Temple—we are required to take care of it and preserve it in purity!

You and I and every Born-Again, Spirit-Filled Believer are the Living Stones building the Eternal House in which God dwells! Revelation 19:6-8 says,

> *Then I heard what sounded like a great multitude, like the roar of rushing waters and like loud peals of thunder, shouting: "Hallelujah!*

For our Lord God Almighty reigns. Let us rejoice and be glad and give him glory! For the wedding of the Lamb has come, and his bride has made herself ready. Fine linen, bright and clean, was given her to wear." (Fine linen stands for the righteous acts of the saints.)

To me this is very interesting; the Marriage of the Church to Jesus Christ has been and continues to be a time of great rejoicing but what stands out to me is the fact the Bible declares that it was/is the Bride who has made Herself ready. She prepares Her own clothing and it clearly states that the clothing [fine linen] stands for the *righteous acts* or righteousness of the Saints! Ephesians 6:10-13 says,

Finally, be strong in the Lord and in his mighty power. Put on the full armour of God so that you can take your stand against the devil's schemes. For our struggle is not against flesh and blood, but against the rulers, against the authorities, against the powers of this dark world and against the spiritual forces of evil in the heavenly realms. Therefore put on the full armour of God, so that when the day of evil comes, you may be able to stand your ground, and after you have done everything, to stand.

This final picture of the Church as the Army of God is such a contrast from the Church as The Bride of Christ! In this passage not only the concept of warfare is revealed but Apostle Paul warns Believers that we will most certainly face battles. He encourages putting on the entire armour of God to be able to stand in "the evil day"; the day of affliction, testing and satanic pressures. It is obvious, what kind of person puts on armour?—A soldier! The picture painted here by Apostle Paul was closely based on the battle gear of the Roman legionary in his time of writing. The Church is being compared to a Roman legion, the most effective military unit of the ancient world—one that actually conquered most of the known world for the Roman Empire.

While the term "army" is not applied to the Church in the New Testament, the pages therein are filled with militaristic references and characterizations of Christians as soldiers. For example: 2 Timothy 2:3-4 says,

Endure hardship with us like a good soldier of Christ Jesus. No one serving as a soldier gets involved in civilian affairs—he wants to please his commanding officer.

This passage is explicit: Christians are to serve as good soldiers of Jesus Christ the Anointed One. He is our Recruiter.

The Church as the Army of God is revealed so that we could understand the victory that we have in Jesus Christ and to also reveal that He is a Man of war! Scriptures are clear that this is one of the many dimensions of the Nature of the God we are called to serve—He is a Mighty Man of war! Here are a few of those references to this dimension of God's Nature:

When the Children of Israel were delivered from the tyranny of Pharaoh and Egypt and set out on their journey to the Promised Land; the armies of Egypt decided to try one last attempt to destroy them. At one point the Children of Israel were confronted with an insurmountable situation; the Red Sea was before them and Pharaoh's army behind; with nowhere to go, God performed an awesome miracle of having the Red Sea parted for them to go over on dry land and then sealing back the sea to see the host of Pharaoh's army drowned in the sea! On the other side and fresh from that victory they began to sing this song: Exodus 15:1-3 says,

Then Moses and the children of Israel sang this song to the LORD, and spoke, saying: "I will sing to the LORD, For He has triumphed gloriously! The horse and its rider He has thrown into the sea!" The LORD is my strength and song, And He has become my salvation; He is my God, and I will praise Him; My father's God, and I will exalt Him. The LORD is a man of war; The LORD is His name.

So to the Israelites He was revealed as a Man of war! The Psalmist David goes on to further reveal this to us in the following excerpt from Psalm Chapter 24: Psalm 24:7-10 says,

Lift up your heads, O you gates! And be lifted up, you everlasting doors! And the King of glory shall come in. Who is this King of glory? The LORD strong and mighty, The LORD mighty in battle. Lift up your heads, O you gates! Lift up, you everlasting doors! And

the King of glory shall come in. Who is this King of glory? The LORD of hosts, He is the King of glory.

THE LORD OF HOSTS!

David reveals to us that the King of glory is known as *"the Lord of hosts"*! This designation reveals the warfare nature of God; as this term was borrowed from the Hebrew language.

This was the title used for the Lord as Commander of an army organized for battle. The word *hosts* is derived from the Hebrew word *tsaba* and carries the following shades of meaning: host; military service; war; army; service; labour; forced labour; conflict. This word involves several interrelated ideas: a group; impetus; difficulty; and force. These ideas undergird the general concept of *service* which one does for or under a superior rather than for oneself. Tsaba is usually applied to military service but is sometimes used of work in general [*under or for a superior*].

So the Lord is raising up an Army known as His Church and He is the Commander of the Church leading us into a battle that He has already secured the victory for! For this reason the Apostle Paul told us to put on the entire armour of God.

We the Church of Jesus Christ have been equipped and mandated to do the same! The ability for us to use the Sword of the Spirit which is the Word of God is not limited to mature, grown-up Believers. It is available even to infants, because God has already ordained that out the mouth of babes and infants He has ordained strength to silence the enemy [Psalms 8:2]. So teach your children [and new converts] the Word of God! Let them speak into their situations from a tender age.

This brings us to our next chapter where we would look at the power of innovation.

CHAPTER THREE
MY PONDERINGS ON INNOVATION

I HAVE BEEN PONDERING ON THE WAY WE DO THINGS AND WHY... FOR EXAMPLE DO you know that "our order of church service was started around 1521." We have a worship service, receive the tithes and offering, give the announcements and then preach the Word...

I know, most would say: "if it ain't broke don't break it"—but honestly whether it's broke or not is a good question to pose.

In many circles and instances what we see happening is this— Civilization keeps advancing while the Church remains antiquated...

Good thing the rest of the civilization didn't stop advancing.

Could you imagine what would have happened if civilization had rejected the Printing Press or Cell Phone technology? Saying that they never did it that way before and as such weren't going to change!

Or if they could not accept the aircraft or automobile industry, because they just never did it that way before!

Or even the advance in medical science, and the list can go on and on...

Well this is exactly what goes on in many churches and ministries... we get stuck in these ruts and cannot INNOVATE, because we are so used doing it a particular way... Well I am dedicated to changing that!!!

It has been said, "imitation is the highest form of flattery." Well let me go on to say that many ministries emulate, so hard, one group or stream at the cost of developing their present unique anointing, calling or divine mandate. And just because it is similar... doesn't mean it is to administrate, operate or function in the same way.

We must continue to look for ways to raise up and nurture peoples giftings, who are entrusted to us. We are not to make them carbon copies or extensions of ourselves; but we need to help them flow and function in their unique designs so that they can bear the most fruit for the Kingdom of God... I am fed-up of the mere "copycat syndrome"—do not get me wrong, if what we receive from the Lord resembles someone else, then so be it. But at least we would have known that the Lord gave it to us, and to them and we just did not "copycat it"...

Remember this:

- The Anointing Is Not Obsolete.
- The Blood Didn't Loose Its Power.
- We Don't Have To Compromise The Gospel. (Doctrine, Holiness, Gifts, Etc) But We Must Be INNOVATIVE...
- Jesus Christ Is Still Wanting To Raise Up Different Expressions Of Church and Ministry That Is Not Antiquated.

We must be willing to recognize, train, develop and deploy new means, methods and ministries. Yes it will require we hear direction and input from heaven, you probably won't either.

In consulting with Pastors, I often ask them, do you ever feel the urge or impression to do service in a different way; or to step out in a different way to minister? (Not because you saw it somewhere but because you feel it in your spirit.) 100% of them say yes. However, only about 2% probably, will actually begin to follow the Spirit, feel the freedom, enjoy their uniqueness and enjoy the new harvest.

Most remain in cavemen ministry instead. This could apply to family, business, marriages, eating habits, whatever... lets don't be a undeveloped people, community, nation or Kingdom, in Jesus Name! Let the Church say Amen! 1 Corinthians 12:4-7 gives us a powerful example; here is what it says,

Now there are diversities of gifts, but the same Spirit. And there are differences of administrations, but the same Lord. And there are

diversities of operations, but it is the same God which worketh all in all. But the manifestation of the Spirit is given to every man to profit withal. KJV

Here is a couple more worthy passages: Proverbs 22:6 says,

Train up a child in the way he should go [and in keeping with his individual gift or bent], and when he is old he will not depart from it. AMP

Psalms 46:4

There is a river, the streams [implying many different flows and directions] whereof shall make glad the city of God, the holy place of the tabernacles of the most High. KJV

In our next chapter we will be exploring the author's ponderings on wisdom and the power of vision...

Chapter Four
My Ponderings On Wisdom and The Power of Vision

I HAVE BEEN PONDERING THE WHOLE IDEA OF THE WAY WE DO CHURCH AND THE power of vision and innovation and a couple of things began engaging my attention:

I kept seeing our ministry D-LIM [Dominion-Life International Ministries] doing a flash mob to Champion [a worship song written by our Worship Team] and other songs at which, we would distribute tracks and flyers to the ministry...

I have also been seeing the vision of D-LIM encapsulated in 7 Pillars and we using those seven Pillars to be the basis for our teaching... Here is what it is:

The Lord has been speaking to me about the following: Proverbs 9:1 says,

Wisdom has built her house, She has hewn out her seven pillars.

Proverbs 24:3-10

Through wisdom a house is built, And by understanding it is established; By knowledge the rooms are filled With all precious and pleasant riches. A wise man is strong, Yes, a man of knowledge increases strength; For by wise counsel you will wage your own

war, And in a multitude of counsellors there is safety. Wisdom is too lofty for a fool; He does not open his mouth in the gate. He who plots to do evil Will be called a schemer. The devising of foolishness is sin, And the scoffer is an abomination to men. If you faint in the day of adversity, Your strength is small.

It's interesting that Proverbs 9:1 mentions seven pillars.

- Pillars are basically for support; they hold the building in place.
- Pillars give the building its strength.

In Scriptures the number "7" is what we would describe as completeness or perfection. The point is that wisdom is a perfect guide for life.

Although Proverbs 9 does not go immediately and give a list of seven specific pillars or components of wisdom, there are principles found in the Book of Proverbs that give us the ability to understand what I call possible pillars that we can use in God's Church to build upon.

WISDOM'S SEVEN PILLARS:

PILLAR ONE: THE FEAR OF THE LORD
Proverbs 9:10 declares,

The fear of the LORD is the beginning of wisdom: and the knowledge of the holy is understanding.

Let's begin with the pillar we describe as probably the main pillar of wisdoms' house.

Fear Of The Lord:

I think we could stop and say that what God wants to see in us are the following:

- An attitude of respect...
- An attitude of awe...
- An attitude of admiration...
- Submission to Him...
- Love for Him.

And I think no doubt all of us can grow in those areas. Proverbs 8:13 declares,

The fear of the LORD is to hate evil; Pride and arrogance and the evil way And the perverse mouth I hate.

So we begin to see that this fear leads us to hate evil, not human beings, but to hate evil. You can love human beings but you don't always love what they do. There are lots of things that human beings do that we just simply shake our head and sometimes wonder. You even feel sad about them; but pride and arrogance and the evil way and the perverse mouth I hate, as prescribe by the Word of God.

PILLAR TWO: KNOWLEDGE AND UNDERSTANDING. Proverbs 18:15 says,

The heart of the prudent [or wise] acquires know-ledge, And the ear of the wise seeks knowledge.

So the heart of the prudent or the wise individual acquires knowledge and the ear of the wise seek knowledge. The Proverbs also tell us: Proverbs 3:13-18 says,

Happy is the man who finds wisdom, And the man who gains understanding; For her proceeds are better than the profits of silver, And her gain than fine gold. She is more precious than rubies, And all the things you may desire cannot compare with her. Length of days is in her right hand, In her left hand riches and honour. Her ways are ways of pleasantness And all her paths are peace. She is tree of life to those who take hold of her, And happy are all who retain her.

In Contrast Let's Look At The Fool: Proverbs 18:2 says,

Fools find no pleasure in understanding but delight in airing their own opinions.
    Fools care nothing for thoughtful discourse; all they do is run off at the mouth. MSG

A [self-confident] fool has no delight in understanding but only in revealing his personal opinions and himself. AMP

- So we recognize that a fool does not find joy in under-standing, but only in expressing his/her own opinion.
- We all have opinions; we all need to have a strong desire to gain understanding rather than just to express our opinions.
- We need to be learning to express God's opinion, not just our own when we're asking for input. I think that's an important thing.

PILLAR THREE: SEEKING GOOD COUNSEL OR ADVICE.
Here are a couple of relevant Scriptures on this: Proverbs 11:14 says,

Where there is no counsel, the people fall; but in the multitude of counsellors there is safety. KJV

Proverbs 15:22

Plans fail for lack of counsel, but with many advisers they succeed.

Please Understand This:

- Seeking advice is not asking or allowing someone else to make your decision!
- Seeking advice and counsel is checking to see if our analysis is correct!
- It is checking to see if our plan is sound.
- Many times counsel gives us a different perspective and more options to consider.
- If your analysis is good you'll have more confidence after getting counsel to move ahead.

PILLAR FOUR: FORESIGHT

- Foresight is the ability to look beyond the immediate situation and to see the end result.

- A wise person thinks about the effect and the outcome of his actions and he avoids a lot of heartache and he avoids a lot of suffering.

I like what Catherine Pulsifer said: "When you find yourself stressed, ask yourself one question: Will this matter in 5 years from now? If yes, then do something about the situation. If no, then let it go."

Proverbs 27:12 provide a very important principle that has to do with foresight. It says,

A prudent man foresees the evil and hides himself but the simple pass on and are punished.

PILLAR FIVE: ACCEPTING CORRECTION

Learning to accept and to welcome correction is an important theme of the Book of Proverbs and of the entire Bible. But it is extremely hard for most of us to do.

Proverbs 3:11 in the NIV says,

My son, do not reject the Lords discipline and do not resent His rebuke; because the Lord disciplines those He loves and as a father a son in whom he delights.

And in Hebrews 12:11 it states,

No discipline seems pleasant at the time, but painful. Later on, however, it produces a harvest of righteousness and peace for those who have been trained by it.

Correction Is Neither Easy Nor Pleasant:

We need to be willing to admit that we are only human and we make mistakes and we fall short.

- You can pray.
- You can study your Bible.
- You can fast.
- But you have to also ask God for correction.

Remember what the Prophet Jeremiah said: Jeremiah 10:24 says,

O Lord, correct, instruct, and chastise me, but with judgment and in just measure--not in Your anger, lest You diminish me and bring me to nothing. AMP

Correct me, but please be fair, don't correct me when You're angry otherwise you will reduce me to nothing. GWT

And in Proverbs 12:1, it states,

Whosoever loves instruction, loves knowledge, but he who hates correction is stupid.

I think you'll find that's basically what we have to realize.

PILLAR SIX: SELF-DISCIPLINE OR SELF-CONTROL
There is a high price that is paid for acquiring wisdom. Prayer, Bible study and fasting of course takes a lot of self-discipline doesn't it? Knowing what is right is one thing, doing it is another.

This is how the Book of Proverbs launches out in the New Century Version. Proverbs 1:1-6 says,

These are the wise words of Solomon son of David, king of Israel. They teach wisdom and self-control; [or self-discipline] they will help you understand wise words. They will teach you how to be wise and self-controlled and will teach you to do what is honest and fair and right. They make the uneducated wise and give knowledge and sense to the young. Wise people can also listen and learn; even they can find good advice in these words. Then anyone can understand wise words and stories, the words of the wise and their riddles.

Proverbs teach wisdom and self-control...The NIV calls this, instead of self-control, discipline. The Hebrew word actually does mean discipline in the sense of the word of disciplining yourself...

Verse 3—They will teach you how to be wise and to be self-controlled/disciplined and will teach you to do what is honest and fair and right.

SELF-DISCIPLINE IS AN ESSENTIAL QUALITY OF CHRISTIANS.
It is a requirement in the list of qualifications for leaders in Paul's letters of both Timothy and Titus.

We are seeking to build a ministry full of leaders and as such we all will have to ultimately come under those qualifications for Elders.

- The measure of a man or a woman is based on these qualities, it really is.
- These are things that we ALL must come to…
- They're not just for Elders to be ordained, but they are for all of us to become kings and priests.
- It has always been God's desire to establish a Kingdom of Priests [A Royal Priesthood]…

1 Timothy 3:1-7

What I say is true: Anyone wanting to become an overseer desires a good work. An overseer must not give people a reason to criticize him, and he must have only one wife. He must be self-controlled, wise, respected by others, ready to welcome guests, and able to teach. He must not drink too much wine or like to fight, but rather be gentle and peaceable, not loving money. He must be a good family leader, having children who cooperate with full respect. (If someone does not know how to lead the family, how can that person take care of God's church?) But an elder must not be a new believer, or he might be too proud of himself and be judged guilty just as the devil was. An elder must also have the respect of people who are not in the church so he will not be criticized by others and caught in the devil's trap. NCV

Titus 1:5-9

I left you in Crete so you could finish doing the things that still needed to be done and so you could appoint elders in every town, as I directed you. An elder must not be guilty of doing wrong, must have only one wife, and must have believing children. They must not be known as children who are wild and do not cooperate. As

God's managers, overseers must not be guilty of doing wrong, being selfish, or becoming angry quickly. They must not drink too much wine, like to fight, or try to get rich by cheating others. Overseers must be ready to welcome guests, love what is good, be wise, live right, and be holy and self-controlled. By holding on to the trustworthy word just as we teach it, overseers can help people by using true teaching, and they can show those who are against the true teaching that they are wrong. NCV

Notice the advice/instruction given by the Apostle Paul in 2 Timothy 2:24 I like how the God's Word translation states it. It says,

A servant of the Lord must not quarrel, instead he must be kind to everyone, he must be a good teacher, he must be willing to suffer wrong, he must be gentle in correcting those who oppose the good news. GWT

PILLAR SEVEN: DEVELOPING AND MAINTAINING GOOD RELATIONSHIPS
- Good people skills are very necessary in service...
- They are very necessary as kings and priests...
- They are very necessary in dealing with the world in which we live and for every generation...

So Much Of Having Wisdom Involves:

- Having good human relationships...
- Valuing other people...
- Learning to apply the laws of loving your neighbour as yourself...

A Foolish Person, On The Other Hand:

- Is so self-centred and self-absorbed that he/she doesn't consider the feelings of others...
- Doesn't consider the needs of other people...

• He/she puts a strain on relationships...
• Unnecessarily offends other people and pushes that person away...

Apostle James says the following in James 3:17

Wisdom from above is first pure, then peaceable, gentle, willing to yield, full of mercy and good fruits without partiality and without hypocrisy.

RECAP: WISDOM SEVEN PILLARS FROM PROVERBS:

1. The Fear Of The Lord
2. Knowledge And Understanding (Present Truth)
3. Seeking Good Counsel Or Advice
4. Foresight
5. Accepting Correction
6. Self-Discipline Or Self-Control
7. Developing And Maintaining Good Relationship

WISDOM'S SEVEN PILLARS ACCORDING TO APOSTLE JAMES:

Finally, Apostle James gives us another great angle or overview of Wisdom's Seven Pillars: Here is what he said: James 3:13-18 says,

Who is there among you who is wise and intelligent? Then let him by his noble living show forth his [good] works with the [unobtrusive] humility [which is the proper attribute] of true wisdom. But if you have bitter jealousy (envy) and contention (rivalry, selfish ambition) in your hearts, do not pride yourselves on it and thus be in defiance of and false to the Truth. This [superficial] wisdom is not such as comes down from above, but is earthly, unspiritual (animal), even devilish (demoniacal). For wherever there is jealousy (envy) and contention (rivalry and selfish ambition), there will also be confusion (unrest, disharmony, rebellion) and all sorts of evil and vile practices. But the wisdom from above is first of all pure (undefiled); then it is peace-loving, courteous (considerate, gentle).

[It is willing to] yield to reason, full of compassion and good fruits; it is wholehearted and straightforward, impartial and unfeigned (free from doubts, wavering, and insincerity). And the harvest of righteousness (of conformity to God's will in thought and deed) is [the fruit of the seed] sown in peace by those who work for and make peace [in themselves and in others, that peace which means concord, agreement, and harmony between individuals, with undisturbedness, in a peaceful mind free from fears and agitating passions and moral conflicts]. AMPC [Parenthesis added]

Verse 17 gives us the seven pillars: *But the wisdom that is from above is first pure, then peaceable, gentle, and easy to be entreated, full of mercy and good fruits, without partiality and without hypocrisy.*

WISDOM'S SEVEN PILLARS FROM APOSTLE JAMES:

1. *Purity*
2. *Peaceable*
3. *Gentleness*
4. *Reasonableness* ("easy to be entreated")
5. *Helpfulness* ("full of mercy and good fruits,")
6. *Humility* ("without partiality")
7. *Sincerity*

Therefore, a life of genuine wisdom is a life founded upon the fear of the Lord and supported by genuine purity, peaceableness, gentleness, reasonableness, helpfulness, humility, and sincerity. Such a house will never fall!

In the next chapter we would be looking at the author's ponderings on navigating seasons of transition.

CHAPTER FIVE
MY PONDERINGS ON NAVIGATING SEASONS OF TRANSITION

I AM CONVINCED BEYOND MEASURE THAT THE EVENTS OF THE PAST WHILE ARE indicators of open windows of opportunity to tap into God's enabling grace that will equip us to run the full course of our apostolic/prophetic journey. The Holy Spirit will work within our hearts until our will is aligned to His will and our thoughts to His. God will also release upon us the needed grace to do what He has instructed us to do.

God in His mercy brings our will and mind into obedience to His desires. He will also release His strength, provision, and wisdom to accomplish His revealed will.

Philippians 2:12-13 declares this to us, it says,

So then, my beloved, just as you have always obeyed, not as in my presence only, but now much more in my absence, work out your salvation with fear and trembling; for it is God who is at work in you, both to will and to work for His good pleasure.

The enabling grace that is released upon us as the Holy Spirit works in us will make us sufficient ministers and vessels of honour.

And in Ephesians 3:7-9 we read about God's amazing grace: here is what it says,

Of which I was made a minister, according to the gift of God's grace which was given to me according to the working of His power. [8]To me, the very least of all saints, this grace was given, to preach to the Gentiles the unfathomable riches of Christ, and to bring to light what is the administration of the mystery which for ages has been hidden in God, who created all things Jesus Christ.

This enabling grace will release upon us the wisdom necessary to administer His will until it is fully executed, bringing glory to His Name. When such apostolic wisdom is manifested in His Church, the powers of darkness will be apprehended and subdued. This will further extend God's Kingdom and advance His purposes that He has brought about in Christ. Ephesians 3:10-11 says,

In order that the manifold wisdom of God might now be made known through the church to the rulers and the authorities in the heavenly places. This was in accordance with the eternal purpose which He carried out in Christ Jesus our Lord,

A sense of prophetic urgency compels me to challenge every one of us **To Be Vigilant And Discerning,** Matthew 24:4 says,

And Jesus answered and said to them, "See to it that no one [misleads] deceives you." [Parenthesis added]

In this teaching we will seek to cover all the dangers that we could/would face in this our current transition from now and on into the future.

WHAT IS TRANSITION?

- Transition time is the time between receiving the promise and seeing its fulfilment.
- This transition is the time of waiting for God's salvation to be made manifest, when all the right conditions are fulfilled and all the right commands are obeyed.
- The transition time is the time of testing our faith and character to see if we will believe His Word and trust Him fully in obedience, finding true confidence in Him.

- The transition time is the time when God will intervene in the affairs of men and realign them to His ultimate plans, redirecting them into His predetermined will in total obedience.
- The transition time is the time when God will cause all things to work together for good for those that love Him and are called according to His purposes. Romans 8:28 declares,

And we know that God causes all things to work together for good to those who love God, to those who are called according to His purpose.

God is leading us in these transition times until we have come into the fullness of all that He has promised in and through this House, Dominion-Life International Ministries, and the many other houses across the earth that are experiencing this kind of transition!

However, I Believe That There Are Dangers To Beware Of In This Journey As We Stride Towards Our Destiny.

THE DANGER OF ABORTING OUR PROPHETIC JOURNEY
In Genesis 11:31 it says,

And Terah took Abram his son, and Lot, the son of Haran, his son's son, and Sarai his daughter-in-law, his son Abram's wife. And he went forth with them from Ur of the Chaldees, to go into the land of Canaan. And they came to Haran and lived there.

Obviously Terah, Abraham's father, heard from God that he was to leave the Ur of the Chaldeans and journey into Canaan, the Promised Land; but he went as far as Haran and settled there.

THE SCRIPTURE IS CLEAR THAT TERAH DIED IN THE PLACE WHERE HE CHOSE TO SETTLE.

And the days of Terah were two hundred and five years; and Terah died in Haran. Genesis 11:32

So many of us are good starters of a journey but do not have the grace to finish. It requires spiritual energy and 'pit-bull' type of tenacity to leave the Ur of the Chaldean [whatever that place is for you] in order to enter in the land of promise! Many men would settle down at an obstacle or because of another person's intimidation.

Whatever the reason, we are not made to settle for less than the Lord's best.

In Matthew 8:28, we read that two demon-possessed men sat at a road in the country of the Gadarenes and prevented anyone from passing that way. They were so extremely violent that no one could pass that way for fear of being harmed. Here it what it says,

> And when He had come to the other side into the country of the Gergesenes, two demon-possessed ones met Him, coming out of the tombs, exceedingly fierce, so that no one might pass by that way.

WHAT ARE THE DEMONS THAT ARE HINDERING YOU?

There are so many 'NO GO ZONES' the devil will place on this journey against those who are walking in this apostolic move. They may be sternly warning us to be quiet and control our passion and ourselves; but if we remain silent at such a time as this, we may forfeit our destiny. We cannot abort our prophetic journey. Luke 18:39 says,

> And those who led the way were sternly telling him to be quiet; but he kept crying out all the more, "Son of David, have mercy on me!"

Esther 4:14

> For if you remain silent at this time, relief and deliverance will arise for the Jews from another place and you and your father's house will perish. And who knows whether you have not attained royalty for such a time as this?

Terah means to tarry, stop at, or wait and linger around. If we tarry when God wants us to move forward to the next level, we will become stagnant in our spiritual walk. Every 'no go zone' of the devil must be challenged and we must breakthrough to the finish.

SECURE ACCURATE ALLIANCES

In 2 Kings 3, we read of the prophetic guidance that Elisha gave to king Jehoram [son of Ahab and Jezebel] of Israel and king Jehoshaphat of Judah for their battle against Moab. The king of Edom also came into alliance with them. King Jehoram's negative words and confession were already conditioning their minds and determining their destiny.

Remember that the Israelites who comprised of 12 tribes had split with 10 tribes [Reuben, Dan, Naphtali, Gad, Asher, Issachar, Zebulun, Ephraim, (western) Manasseh and (eastern) Manasseh in Gilead] forming the Northern Kingdom of Israel and the other 2 tribes [Judah and Benjamin] the Southern Kingdom of Judah... While the Edomites are descendants of Esau; Isaac's son: 2 Kings 3:10, 14 says,

> *Then the king of Israel said, "Alas! For the LORD has called these three kings to give them into the hand of Moab." ... And Elisha said, "As the LORD of hosts lives, before whom I stand, were it not that I regard the presence of Jehoshaphat the king of Judah, I would not look at you nor see you."*

We need to be sure that those who are in alliance with us are not programmed for defeat in their minds and in their soul. We must align ourselves to God's prophetic words. King Jehoshaphat quickly re-established their spiritual position by seeking God's word to build his destiny and future outcome: 2 Kings 3:11-14 says,

> *And Jehoshaphat said, Is there not here a prophet of Jehovah, that we may ask of Jehovah by him? And one of the king of Israel's servants answered and said, Here is Elisha the son of Shaphat, who poured water on the hands of Elijah. And Jehoshaphat said, The Word of Jehovah is with him. And the king of Israel, and Jehoshaphat, and the king of Edom went down to him. And Elisha said to the king of Israel, What do I have to do with you? Go to the prophets of your father and to the prophets of your mother. And the king of Israel said to him, No, for Jehovah has called these three kings together to deliver them into the hand of Moab. And Elisha said, As Jehovah of Hosts lives, before whom I stand, surely if it were not that I regard the presence of Jehoshaphat the king of Judah, I would not look toward you nor see you.*

KING JEHOSHAPHAT'S ALLIANCE WITH THE PROPHET ELISHA BROUGHT A MEASURE OF VICTORY

The Prophet Elisha gave them a clear strategy for total victory: a complete destruction of the cities, the trees, the water, and the fields. The three kings executed the strategy and saw tremendous victory.

"NO GO ZONES" THAT WERE NOT DEALT WITH RE-SURFACES DURING ACTIVE WARFARE

But when the king of Moab saw that he was cornered on all sides, he began to press towards the south against Edom while Israel pursued them into Moab territory.

The king of Moab then sacrificed his oldest son, who was to reign in his place, upon the walls of the city. This act was a demonic worship ritual that caused demonic powers to be released upon Israel, who was pursuing them. These powers of the air came in great wrath and sent the Israelites out in confusion. The Israelites departed from attacking the king of Moab, and returned to their own land without finishing the prophetic journey to total victory. The Israelites did not know what hit them, as it was spiritual powers of the air.

BEWARE OF DEMONIC DISTRACTIONS IN FULFILLING YOUR DESTINY AND PURPOSE IN LIFE

Sometimes when we begin on a prophetic quest with God's word and direction, the enemy can distract us or bring us into confusion. We must not rest until the journey is done.

Spiritual powers can create '**No Go Zones**' in our lives and prevent us from moving on in God. Don't abort the prophetic journey. Stay in total obedience to the word. Stay connected to the prophetic/apostolic source so that progressive revelations can revive and renew your strength on the journey.

THE POWER OF THE RESIDENT ANOINTING ESTABLISHED THROUGH ACCURATE ALLIANCES

In 2 Kings 4:1-7, we read the following account, which says,

A certain woman of the wives of the sons of the prophets cried out to Elisha, saying, "Your servant my husband is dead, and you know

that your servant feared the LORD. And the creditor is coming to take my two sons to be his slaves." So Elisha said to her, "What shall I do for you? Tell me, what do you have in the house?" And she said, "Your maidservant has nothing in the house but a jar of oil." Then he said, "Go, borrow vessels from everywhere, from all your neighbors—empty vessels; do not gather just a few. And when you have come in, you shall shut the door behind you and your sons; then pour it into all those vessels, and set aside the full ones." So she went from him and shut the door behind her and her sons, who brought the vessels to her; and she poured it out. Now it came to pass, when the vessels were full, that she said to her son, "Bring me another vessel." And he said to her, "There is not another vessel." So the oil ceased. Then she came and told the man of God. And he said, "Go, sell the oil and pay your debt; and you and your sons live on the rest."

Here we see the widow of one of the sons of the prophets going to the original prophetic source and asking Elisha for help. If the word of God has sustained us thus far, it will sustain us also in the future. Elisha's word not only saved her sons from the creditors, but they also were able to pay their debt and have money left over for the rest of their lives. The prophetic/apostolic journey and call can be stopped by various circumstances, including death.

ANOTHER INTERESTING ACCOUNT
In the story of the Shunammite woman, you can read the full account in 2 Kings 4:8-37, however, let us read the following verses, 2 Kings 4:8-11, which says,

And the day came when Elisha passed over to Shunem. And a great woman was there. And she laid hold on him to eat bread. And it happened, as often as he passed by, he turned in there to eat bread. And she said to her husband, Behold now, I see that this is a holy man of God who passes by us continually. Please, let us make a little room on the wall. And let us set a bed for him there, and a table, and a stool, and a lampstand. And when he comes to us, he shall turn in there. And the day came when he came in there, and he turned into the room and lay there.

We see how she became connected to the prophetic when Elisha passed by that area. She persuaded her husband, and together they built for him a walled, upper chamber in their house.

WHEN THE PROPHETIC IS NO LONGER A "PASSERBY" IN OUR LIFE, BUT A "RESIDENT ANOINTING,"

We will see significant changes in our lives. God not only blessed her and her husband, but also blessed the second generation. She received a son.

When God's word becomes the primary source for the things happening in our lives, then His word alone can carry us on to the next level. In our prophetic/apostolic journey of going from one level to another, the enemy can try to destroy that which was begun by the spirit. We need to go back to God's original word and primary source and reactivate the wells of our fathers.

When her child died of sunstroke, the Shunammite woman took the dead body and placed him upon Elisha's bed and sought for him until she found him. She tapped into the same prophetic anointing she had become acquainted with. She had already learned the power of God's prophetic words and had seen its effect upon her body and her husband's. She understood that the prophetic anointing could release

God's healing power to restore the physical body.

When the enemy tries to rob or destroy what God has released upon us by His word, we need to go back to God's original word and into His presence and dig into the same well of His supply for strength to rise above these attacks.

It takes one level of battle to win and to breakthrough, and yet another level of warfare to maintain what we have won in the Spirit. God is teaching us in this transition time not to abort our prophetic/apostolic journey, come "hell or high water" [regardless to whatever happens]. We must be determined to cross the finishing line. We must, without compromise, press towards the final end, into our destiny.

Let us now turn our gaze and ponder on breakthroughs!

Chapter Six
My Ponderings on Breakthroughs

FREEDOM/LIBERTY—IS NOT NECESSARILY THE ABSENCE OF PRESSURE, STRESS OR opposition! It is a conscious position we take. It is not the freedom, nor the ability to do whatsoever comes to mind, nor to fill whatever pleasure or sensuality sought after by the flesh. It is a state of INNER BEING that is submitted and led by the Holy Spirit! —Remember, *who the Son sets free, is free indeed*... John 8:36

Give me liberty or give me death! That is what Jesus Christ came to do—give us liberty! So that is why the Scriptures declare—"*He who the Son sets FREE is FREE indeed*". Enjoy your freedom in Christ and do NOT become entangled with the yoke of bondage and live-in habitual sin

The world's system is designed to "train or school" us to serve it and to lose sight of the true realm of the Kingdom of God. Music, Culture, Economics, Politics, etc are all designed to "train" us! It is designed to cause us to become 'numbed' to Kingdom values and principles. We MUST seek to advance God's Kingdom instead of surrendering to the systems of this world!

An apostolic trait that defines the authority of Jesus Christ—the Sender—is the ability to identify breaches and possess them. It is when one can identify a breach and then take possession of that breach then breakthrough happens. In other words, the "Possessor of the Breach" becomes the "Master of Breakthroughs"—names that are associated with God as found in 2 Samuel 5:20, which says,

> *So David went to Baal Perazim, and David defeated them there; and he said, "The LORD has broken through my enemies before me, like a breakthrough of water." Therefore he called the name of that place Baal Perazim.*

Possessing a breach allows the possessor to enforce "shibboleth" [Judges 12:6] and control incoming and outgoing traffic; possessing the breach allows one to repair the breach; possessing the breach allows a re-exertion of authority over areas previously ravaged and brings about a transformation of the realm.

Be it our individual lives or the corporate body, breakthroughs may be effected by possessing the breaches that have often been used by the devil to ravage, affect, harass or impoverish our lives. Scripture provides insight as to how we can deliberately accelerate breakthroughs

In Zechariah 8:18-19 for instance, you find an example of breaches being transformed as God promises His people that He would turn the fasts of the fourth, fifth, seventh and tenth months into feasts. Here is what it says,

> *And the Word of Jehovah of Hosts came to me, saying, So says Jehovah of Hosts: The fast of the fourth month, and the fast of the fifth, and the fast of the seventh, and the fast of the tenth, shall be to the house of Judah for joy and gladness, and cheerful feasts. Therefore love truth and peace.*

If fasts are seen as a time of mourning and lament, then feasts are a reversal of privation, famine and grief. In fact, these fasts were ordered to remember the siege, devastation, rebellion and fall of Jerusalem as outlined in 2 Kings 25.

The fast of the fourth month remembered the breaking down of the walls of Jerusalem. For this fast to be converted to a time of feasting, it would require that the walls be rebuilt. Very often in our walk here on earth when walls have been broken down and life has been hijacked or ransacked by events or forces, the re-building of walls is impossible till we withdraw from blaming God or casting suspicion on His nature or holding Him responsible for what has happened. Time and again when Israel went through situations that were hard, they prevented God from showing His mighty arm of power by immediately blaming Him for their woes. While we may not use the words that Israel used, our heart condition may speak louder before God than the usage of words. At one point, even Jeremiah was cautioned by God when He addressed God as being like a deceptive brook. In Jeremiah 15:19, God warns Him that should he not cease from casting suspicion on the character of God, that God would stop using Jeremiah as His mouthpiece or spokesman. Take heed, lest you and I fall into the same pattern and find ourselves unable to lay the foundation required to re-build the wall.

The fast of the fifth month was to remember the destruction of the temple. The feast then would signify the rebuilding of the temple. Given that our bodies are the temple of the Holy Spirit, it necessitates my handing over the keys to all the rooms of my life so that the Master may drive out, cleanse and occupy the premise of my life at will.

Rebuilding the temple of my life requires that I begin to inspect not the fruit but the root systems in my life. Often times, we fall into the trap of purging offensive and rotting fruit in our lives on a consistent but repetitive basis when what is really called for is an eradication of the offensive root so that putrid fruit production may cease. While God is willing to forgive the sinful fruit of our lives He would much rather have access to deal with the sinful root in our lives.

The fast of the seventh month remembered the rebellion against the God-ordained reign of Gedaliah who was later murdered [2 Kings 25:25]. The feast would then require a return to submission under divinely structured authority and covering.

Given the rights-oriented climate and culture in which, we now live, rebellion is a state of being that has begun to permeate church, family and individual lives. Rebellion is not an armed uprising, or a church split or dissension. It is the active state of "being an authority unto oneself".

The Kingdom however has always operated on the code of "submission to authority" and the principle of "first among equals" as seen even in the Godhead with Father, Son and Spirit being co-equal and yet the Father being first among equals. Similarly, in the appointment of the five offices, Apostles rank first (proton) among equals; in a family, even though husband and wife are equal, the man is first among equals and so on. When this structure is baulked in the church, hell literally breaks loose.

As much as God's angels minister and protect the Saints submitted to the Lordship of Christ, rebellion, usurping control and the casting off of restraints allows room for demonic forces (fallen angels) to ravish the body—a condition that fallen angels are very familiar with and quick to exploit—given that it was their rebellion in God's backyard that had them cast out of the heavens.

Continuing the same line of thought, I would suggest that given the patriarchal nature of societies in pre-Noahic times of Genesis 6, it is improbable that fallen angels could have had as they pleased, the daughters of men, had it not been for a state of rebellion and a casting off of covering and restraint. The call then is to deliberately and at all cost return to living under divinely ordained structure in every area of my life.

The fast of the tenth month—was to remember the siege and beginning of the reign of an Assyrian king that would be accompanied by famine, captivity and restriction of the worship of the God of Israel. The feast would then be signified by an abundance of revelation, teaching of the Word, knowledge of the will of God, the reign of Christ on earth as it is in heaven, abandon in worship and progress from the wells of Rehoboth to the wells of Beersheba [Genesis 26].

It requires a deliberate decision to increase my intake of all that is God-breathed, just as an athlete tailors his diet, his habits, his training, attitude and choices so that peak performance may be attained both at the start and finish lines.

Once these breaches are taken and the fasts are converted to feasts, we need to plan for breakthrough. The first step towards breakthrough is to be able to discern the nature of the enemy's attacks and the weapons he wields.

If we were to take Goliath (*whose name means to denude or strip away*) as an archetype of the enemy, an inspection of the weapons he carried reveals the wiles that the devil normally uses against the saints of God.

Goliath's weapons included the *kidon*—or the sickle—that is used to destroy the harvest after much hard work (read Judges 6:3-6), suffocating and sapping the will to continue; the *chereb* or the sword—which is used indiscriminately in a torrent of slashes and blows that come wave after wave as with Job (Job 1:13-22), breaking the spirit; the javelin—used in pre-emptive strikes by the enemy for long-distance hurling to take out that which is God-birthed even before it comes to fruition—as the devil tried to do with both Moses and Jesus. This is a ploy that is particularly used against apostolic houses.

A second prototype we should look at is Balaam *(to conquer a people)*. Dissecting the schemes of this diviner reveals other strategies the devil employs. Initially Balaam used a frontal attack on the Israelites as a means to affect their destiny (Numbers chapters 22 and 23). He harnessed forces that he was familiar with to do them harm—just as satan harnessed forces against Job to do him harm. When a frontal assault failed because of God's intervention—Balaam resorted to the Trojan attack—a highly successful device that the enemy still uses against our lives. What Balaam failed to achieve by cursing Israel he accomplished through seduction (Numbers 25), sending Moabite women to seduce the men of Israel. Be warned of back-door breaches particularly after you have withstood a frontal assault.

Once the enemy's manoeuvres are exposed, breakthroughs are established by taking divine initiative, being resourceful and pressing home the advantage that we possess in God unlike King Joash (2 Kings 13:14-20) who struck the ground just three times at the prophet's command. Maters of breakthrough do not operate like that they press the advantage gained on the enemy. Here are some of the qualities of these Kingdom-minded people, which we would describe as "Masters of Breakthrough!"

Masters of Breakthrough do not always wait for the battle to come to their doorstep but at times, they provoke hostilities (Numbers 25:16) and initiate pre-emptive strikes against the enemy as God reveals plots in advance. They are aware that the serpent's head has been crushed under the heel of Jesus. A head crushed serpent can still writhe and look deadly but its fangs are broken and its time is limited.

Masters of Breakthrough have the understanding and the ability to declare upon the enemy confusion, darkness, dullness, a lack of understanding and restriction of activity as befell Pharaoh and his armies at the Red Sea and as is the present state of spirit beings held in Tartarus: Exodus 14:19-21 says,

And the Angel of God, who went before the camp of Israel, moved and went behind them; and the pillar of cloud went from before them and stood behind them. So it came between the camp of the Egyptians and the camp of Israel. Thus it was a cloud and darkness to the one, and it gave light by night to the other, so that the one did not come near the other all that night. Then Moses stretched out his hand over the sea; and the LORD caused the sea to go back by a strong east wind all that night, and made the sea into dry land, and the waters were divided.

2 Peter 2:4

For if God did not spare the angels who sinned, but cast them down to hell and delivered them into chains of darkness, to be reserved for judgment.

Masters of Breakthrough can stop the enemy's use of the elements of nature to harm the Saints of God. satan often uses facets of nature, as with Job, also Jesus (wind & waves), to sabotage lives. Just as Jesus took authority over the wind, we to can stop the devil from exploiting created order. Like Joshua, who told the sun to stand still, we to could harness the elements of nature until the route of the enemy is complete.

Masters of Breakthrough can stop the enemy's use of the elements to harm the Saints of God. satan often uses facets of nature, as with Job, also Jesus (wind and waves), to sabotage lives. Just as Jesus took authority over the wind, we to can stop the devil from exploiting created order. Like Joshua who told the sun to stand still, we to could harness the elements of nature until the route of the enemy is complete

Masters of Breakthrough locate and engages the source, not the offshoots. 1 Samuel 17 reveals that David was not alone on the battlefield with Goliath but that there was also Goliath's shield-bearer who walked ahead of him, carrying his heavy shield. Often we battle the shield-bearer who is dispensable and is continuously replaced when we should be attacking the main source behind the shield-bearer.

Judges 8:4 reveals that "When Gideon came to the Jordan, he and the three hundred men who were with him crossed over, exhausted but still in pursuit". This is the awesome power of Momentum, what a tremendous account these men did not regard their tiredness because they gained momentum and did not cease until the job was done! Do not loose momentum in what the Lord has assigned you to do, keep pressing forward! Breakthrough is yours! Break-through is ours!

Onward we go, let's now take a look at some of the author's Ponderings on Unity. Because unity is very significant and vital for us if we are to experience this level of breakthrough!

CHAPTER SEVEN
MY PONDERINGS ON UNITY

THE SPIRIT AND POWER OF AGREEMENT IS A TREMENDOUS DIMENSION FOR powerful, breakthrough prayer that releases the Purpose of God. As we explore the Book of Acts we see some tremendous examples of the Early Church entering into this awesome power that released a powerful synergy as they came into active and deliberate oneness. Here are some references: Acts 1:14 says,

These all continued with one accord in prayer and supplication, with the women and Mary the mother of Jesus, and with His brothers.

Acts 2:1

When the Day of Pentecost had fully come, they were all with one accord in one place.

Acts 2:46

So continuing daily with one accord in the temple, and breaking bread from house to house, they ate their food with gladness and simplicity of heart.

Acts 4:24

So when they heard that, they raised their voice to God with one accord and said: "Lord, You are God, who made heaven and earth and the sea, and all that is in them."

Acts 5:12

And through the hands of the apostles many signs and wonders were done among the people. And they were all with one accord in Solomon's Porch.

Acts 15:25

it seemed good to us, being assembled with one accord, to send chosen men to you with our beloved Barnabas and Paul.

One of the strategies of the enemy is to observe and wait for a suitable target, much like a pride of lions as they hunt a herd of gazelle. The enemy singles out a weak member who will be easier to overcome. This particular animal at some point is separated from the herd just enough so that the lions have room to manoeuvre. This means that the herd is then vulnerable as the prey is overcome and panic ensues causing the herd to scatter and break their tight knit formation.

In the local church and in the Body of Christ, the same strategy is used against us. We have recently seen a high-ranking member of the global Church overtaken by drugs and homosexuality. We as the Body of Christ are still dealing with the after-effects as the enemy tries to use the incident against us. In a local church when a member succumbs to the enemy it can cause fear, doubt, unbelief, and if nothing else a distraction so that we take our eyes off of God. This is all that the enemy needs in order to single out another member and neutralize us one by one.

We were created for such a time as this. This is a critical time for us as a local church in the Body of Christ. We can no longer afford to have an independent mindset or seek after our own vision, or else we will become singled out by the enemy. Here is what Psalms 17:11-12 says,

They have now surrounded us in our steps; They have set their eyes, crouching down to the earth, As a lion is eager to tear his prey, And like a young lion lurking in secret places.

1 Peter 5:8-9

Be sober, be vigilant; because your adversary the devil walks about like a roaring lion, seeking whom he may devour. Resist him, steadfast in the faith, knowing that the same sufferings are experienced by your brotherhood in the world.

If we allow ourselves to be overcome, our absence leaves a void in the defences in which the enemy is able to gain further access to infiltrate and destroy our fellow Saints. John 10:10 says,

The thief does not come except to steal, and to kill, and to destroy.

In order to fulfil all that God has placed before us we must be like the workers re-building the city wall in Jerusalem in Nehemiah 4:13-21, which says,

Therefore I positioned men behind the lower parts of the wall, at the openings; and I set the people according to their families, with their swords, their spears, and their bows. And I looked, and arose and said to the nobles, to the leaders, and to the rest of the people, "Do not be afraid of them. Remember the Lord, great and awesome, and fight for your brethren, your sons, your daughters, your wives, and your houses." And it happened, when our enemies heard that it was known to us, and that God had brought their plot to nothing, that all of us returned to the wall, everyone to his work. So it was, from that time on, that half of my servants worked at construction, while the other half held the spears, the shields, the bows, and wore armor; and the leaders were behind all the house of Judah. Those who built on the wall, and those who carried burdens, loaded themselves so that with one hand they worked at construction, and with the other held a weapon. Every one of the builders had his sword girded at his side as he built. And the one who sounded the trumpet was beside me. Then I said to the nobles, the rulers, and the rest of the people, "The work is great and extensive, and we are separated far from one another on the wall. Wherever you hear the sound of the trumpet, rally to us there. Our God will fight for us." So we labored in the work, and half of the men held the spears from daybreak until the stars appeared.

In order to succeed we must work together as a unified body. Apostle Paul in 1 Corinthians 12:25-26 puts it beautifully; here is what he says,

That there should be no schism in the body, but that the members should have the same care for one another. And if one member suffers, all the members suffer with it; or if one member is honoured, all the members rejoice with it.

Everything we think and everything we do must encompass a "**WE**" mentality. We must continue to work out our own salvation and freely give the benefits to the corporate body. This means that all that we do in our "Christ centred" daily living must have a positive affect in our community and not just in ourselves. Psalms 86:11 says,

Teach me Your way, O Lord, I will walk in Your truth; unite my heart to fear Your name.

Unity is one of our greatest strengths as a people who share one heart and one mind that is solely focused on God. David asks God to unite his heart. In essence what David is asking is for God to ensure that no other allegiances or distractions cause him to stray. It is important to realize that we can construct a corporate expression of one heart and one mind for Christ. 2 Chronicles 30:12 says,

Also the hand of God was on Judah to give them singleness of heart to obey the command of the king and the leaders, at the word of the Lord.

God is the source of unity and He can only grant it when each member is totally "sold out" to Him. This is why unity is so powerful. The Lord commands His blessing where there is unity and together as a unified people we can do more than if we were apart. The following Scriptures gives us some powerful examples of what unity can accomplish.

Psalms 133 says,

Behold, how good and how pleasant it is For brethren to dwell together in unity! It is like the precious oil upon the head, Running down on the beard, The beard of Aaron, Running down on the edge of his garments. It is like the dew of Hermon, Descending upon the mountains of Zion; For there the LORD commanded the blessing— Life forevermore.

Leviticus 26:8

Five of you shall chase a hundred, and a hundred of you shall put ten thousand to flight; your enemies shall fall by the sword before you.

Deuteronomy 32:30

How could one chase a thousand, And two put ten thousand to flight, Unless their Rock had sold them, And the LORD had surrendered them?

Acts 4:32-33

Now the multitude of those who believed were of one heart and soul; neither did anyone say that any of the things he possessed was his own, but they had all things in common. And with great power the apostle gave witness to the resurrection of the Lord Jesus. And great grace was upon them all.

We know that since the Book of Acts was written; the Church has yet to rise up and experience the signs, wonders, and miracles that occurred in that time period. Why are we not currently in that same dimension of great grace? Since that time we have not been able as a body to walk with the same degree of unity. To have one heart and one mind is to be "**in sync**" with one another, and to "**breathe spiritually**" together as one. As the local church comes together in unity and the Body of Christ unites we will see miraculous conversions, signs, wonders and miracles. Acts 2:46-47 says,

> *So continuing daily with one accord in the temple, and breaking bread from house to house, they ate their food with gladness and simplicity of heart, praising God and having favour with all the people. And the Lord added to the church daily those who were being saved.*

Without fully understanding "COVENANT", there can be no forward thrust of God's purpose!

Whenever the Bible illustrates a forward thrust of God's purpose there is always the cutting of covenant to validate the further progression of His divine plan.

COVENANT:

A covenant, in the biblical sense, implies much more than a contract or simple agreement. A contract always has an end date, while a covenant is a permanent arrangement. Another noteworthy difference is that a contract generally involves only one area, such as s skill, while a covenant covers a person's total being.

Covenant is first established between God and man as they commit themselves to partnership for the enforcing of God's divine will upon human civilization. Covenants that are made between God and man extend laterally from man to man as it is necessary for the effective administration and execution of God's purpose.

WHAT IS COVENANT?

A covenant is a contract or a binding agreement between two parties with each party being obligated to the terms and condition of the covenant.

The Hebrew word for Covenant used throughout the Old Testament is *"Berith".* This word is derived from a root word meaning "to cut" in reference to the cutting or dividing of animals into two parts. The parties entering into covenant would pass between the animals. As they walked through the blood, they would bind themselves with a curse that what was done to the animals would be done to them if they violated the terms and conditions of the covenant; clearly illustrated in Genesis 15: 1-21, which says,

> *After these things the word of the* LORD *came to Abram in a vision, saying, "Do not be afraid, Abram. I am your shield, your exceedingly great reward." But Abram said, "Lord* GOD, *what will You give me, seeing I go childless, and the heir of my house is Eliezer of Damascus?" Then Abram said, "Look, You have given me no offspring; indeed one born in my house is my heir!" And behold, the word of the* LORD *came to him, saying, "This one shall not be your heir, but one who will come from your own body shall be your heir." Then He brought him outside and said, "Look now toward heaven, and count the stars if you are able to number them." And He said to him, "So shall your descendants be." And he believed in the* LORD, *and He accounted it to him for righteousness. Then He said to him, "I am the* LORD, *who brought you out of Ur of the Chaldeans, to give you this land to inherit it." And he said, "Lord* GOD, *how shall I know that I will inherit it?" So He said to him, "Bring Me a three-year-old heifer, a three-year-old female goat, a three-year-old ram, a turtledove, and a young pigeon." Then he brought all these to Him and cut them in two, down the middle, and placed each piece opposite the other; but he did not cut the birds in two. And when the vultures came down on the carcasses, Abram drove them away. Now when the sun was going down, a deep sleep fell upon Abram; and behold, horror and great darkness fell upon him. Then He said to Abram: "Know certainly that your descendants will be strangers in a land that is not theirs, and will serve them, and they will afflict them four hundred years. And also the nation whom they serve I will judge; afterward they shall come out with great possessions. Now as for you, you shall go to your fathers in peace; you shall be buried at a good old age. But in the fourth generation they shall return here, for the iniquity of the Amorites is not yet complete." And it came to pass, when the sun went down and it was dark, that behold, there appeared a smoking oven and a burning torch that passed between those pieces. On the same day the* LORD *made a covenant with Abram, saying: "To your descendants I have given this land,*

from the river of Egypt to the great river, the River Euphrates—the Kenites, the Kenezzites, the Kadmonites, the Hittites, the Perizzites, the Rephaim, the Amorites, the Canaanites, the Girgashites, and the Jebusites."

In other words, Covenant is the commitment that lies behind every successful relationship; it comprises the principles of integrity and fidelity; thus guaranteeing the relationship will be preserved and the purpose of that relationship will be realized.

Covenant is not a Christian cliché but it is a pivotal Kingdom characteristic that determines the quality of ones commitment to the Lord and to one another.

PRESERVING THE INTEGRITY OF RELATIONSHIP:
Every relationship entered into by man or woman is a reflection of that person's commitment to an objective that transcends beyond him or herself.

- **Relationship says**—I cannot achieve a mandate alone, but with the pooling of effort, intelligence and resources in other like-minded people will fulfill the mandate. It results in the creation of a corporate mind.
- From that perspective relationships can never be considered mundane and casual. They are not designed to tickle one's emotion or to quell personal loneliness, but rather, relationships are to be used as a currency for the establishment of the Kingdom, which is foundationally grounded in covenant relationships.
- The quality of human relationship depends on the extent of commitment the individual parties have in adhering to the values of covenant. This strict adherence to covenant values is the key feature in protecting the vulnerability of each person within the relationship. Psalms 89:34 says,

I will not break my covenant, nor change the thing that has gone out of my lips.

When God makes covenant and confirms it with an oath, He binds Himself to its fulfillment, making the covenant immutable or unchangeable.

God honours His covenant without annulling and violating the sacredness of it, in spite of the human tendency to fall away, to deny Him, to betray Him and others as we follow after our own sinful ways, God remains faithful.

God's model of faithfulness and integrity should be our standard in relationships. God's standard presents us with the profound principle that along with faithfulness and integrity, covenant relationship is never negated nor is it dependent on the other party's action.

This is the model of Jesus. He gave His life for us even when we were still sinners. This quality of selfless giving must be rekindled in our personal interactions as we aim to fulfill the eternal mandate given to us by the Lord.

There are several covenants mentioned in Scripture:

THE COVENANT WITH NOAH:

When man had become so corrupt in the earth, God found in Noah one who was faithful and able to stand the persecution of the scoffers while working towards the preservation of God's eternal intents. God sealed His commitment to this new initiative with a covenant.

God assured Noah that judgment would not again come to men in the form of a flood; and that the recurrence of the seasons and of day and night should not cease! Please note this was the very first Covenant after creation and so it was very significant!

We read of this in Genesis 9:1-17, it says,

And God blessed Noah and his sons. And He said to them, Be fruitful and multiply, and fill the earth. And the fear of you and the dread of you shall be upon the animals of the earth, and upon every bird of the air, upon all that moves on the earth, and upon all the fish of the sea. Into your hand they are delivered. Every moving thing that lives shall be food for you. I have given you all things, even as the green herb. But you shall not eat of flesh with the life in it or the blood of it. and surely the blood of your lives will I require. At the hand of every animal will I require it, and at the hand of man.

At the hand of every man's brother will I require the life of man. Whoever sheds man's blood, his blood shall be shed by man; for He made man in the image of God. And you be fruitful and multiply. Bring forth abundantly in the earth, and increase in it. And God spoke to Noah, and to his sons with him, saying, Behold! I, even I, establish My covenant with you, and with your seed after you; and with every living creature that is with you, of the birds, of the cattle, and of every animal of the earth with you; from all that go out from the ark, to every animal of the earth. And I will establish My covenant with you. Neither shall all flesh be cut off any more by the waters of a flood. Neither shall there any more be a flood to destroy the earth. And God said, This is the token of the covenant which I make between Me and you and every living creature with you, for everlasting generations: I set my rainbow in the cloud. And it shall be a token of a covenant between Me and the earth. And it shall be, when I bring a cloud over the earth, that the rainbow shall be seen in the cloud. And I will remember My covenant which is between Me and you and every living creature of all flesh; and the waters shall no more become a flood to destroy all flesh. And the rainbow shall be in the cloud. And I will look upon it that I may remember the everlasting covenant between God and every living creature of all flesh that is upon the earth. And God said to Noah, This is the token of the covenant which I have established between Me and all flesh that is upon the earth.

God blessed Noah and his sons and said, "Have many children, so that your descendants will live all over the earth. All the animals, birds, and fish will live in fear of you. They are all placed under your power. Now you can eat them, as well as green plants; I give them all to you for food. The one thing you must not eat is meat with blood still in it; I forbid this because the life is in the blood. If anyone takes human life, he will be punished. I will punish with death any animal that takes a human life. Human beings were made like God, so whoever murders one of them will be killed by someone else. "You must have many children, so that your descendants will live all over the earth." God said to Noah and his sons, "I am now making my covenant with you and with your descendants, and with all living beings---all birds and all animals---everything that came out of the boat with you. With these words I make my covenant with you: I promise that never again will all living beings be destroyed by a flood; never again will a flood destroy the earth. As a sign of this everlasting covenant which I am making with you and with all living beings, I am putting my bow in the clouds. It will be the sign of my covenant with the world. Whenever I cover the sky with clouds and the rainbow appears, I will remember my promise to you and to all the animals that a flood will never again destroy all living beings. When the rainbow appears in the clouds, I will see it and remember the everlasting covenant between me and all living beings on earth. That is the sign of the promise which I am making to all living beings." GNB

Through Noah, the earth was repopulated and God created a nation through whom He could fulfill His redemptive purpose on the earth.

THE COVENANT WITH ABRAHAM:
God chose Abraham who expressed resolute faith in Him! With Abraham, there began the process of building an empowered nation. Again, the signature of God's commitment was the making of a covenant.

Let us read the conditions to the Covenant with Abraham—Genesis 12:1-3, it says,

And Jehovah said to Abram, Go out of your country, and from your kindred, and from your father's house into a land that I will show you. And I will make you a great nation. And I will bless you and make your name great. And you shall be a blessing. And I will bless those that bless you and curse the one who curses you. And in you shall all families of the earth be blessed.

The condition of this covenant was that Abraham was to leave his country, kindred, and father's house, and follow the Lord into the land that He would show him. The promise was a fourfold blessing:

1. He would Increase into a numerous people;
2. There would BE Material and Spiritual Prosperity—"*I will bless you*";

3. That there would be an exaltation of Abraham's name—"*make your name great*";
4. That Abraham was not only to be blessed by God, but also to be a blessing to others.

Later this covenant was renewed, and Abraham was promised a son and abundant posterity. About fourteen years after the making of the covenant it was renewed again, this time with a change of his name and the establishment of circumcision, which was to be the sign of accepting and ratifying the covenant: Genesis 17:1-11 says,

And when Abram was ninety-nine years old, Jehovah appeared to Abram and said to him, I am the Almighty God! Walk before Me and be perfect. And I will make My covenant between Me and you, and will multiply you exceedingly. And Abram fell on his face. And God talked with him, saying, As for Me, behold! My covenant is with you, and you shall be a father of many nations. Neither shall your name any more be called Abram, but your name shall be Abraham. For I have made you a father of many nations. And I will make you exceedingly fruitful, greatly so, and I will make nations of you, and kings shall come out of you. And I will establish My covenant between Me and you and your seed after you in their generations for an everlasting covenant, to be a God to you and to your seed after you. And I will give the land to you in which you are a stranger, and to your seed after you, all the land of Canaan, for an everlasting possession. And I will be their God. And God said to Abraham, And you shall keep My covenant, you and your seed after you in their generations. This is My covenant, which you shall keep, between Me and you and your seed after you. Every male child among you shall be circumcised. And you shall circumcise the flesh of your foreskin. And it shall be a token of the covenant between Me and you.

As God's purpose gained momentum, the baton of responsibility was moved from one faithful partner to another, as Abraham passed it on to Isaac an so on down the line. At every stage of the divine evolution process there was the making of covenant to underscore and validate the progress.

Moses was the next a star pupil as the baton was passed and Moses continued in the way of his fathers as shown in the following passages: Exodus 24:1-8 says,

Now He said to Moses, "Come up to the LORD, you and Aaron, Nadab and Abihu, and seventy of the elders of Israel, and worship from afar. And Moses alone shall come near the LORD, but they shall not come near; nor shall the people go up with him." So Moses came and told the people all the words of the LORD and all the judgments. And all the people answered with one voice and said, "All the words which the LORD has said we will do." And Moses wrote all the words of the LORD. And he rose early in the morning, and built an altar at the foot of the mountain, and twelve pillars according to the twelve tribes of Israel. Then he sent young men of the children of Israel, who offered burnt offerings and sacrificed peace offerings of oxen to the LORD. And Moses took half the blood and put it in basins, and half the blood he sprinkled on the altar. Then he took the Book of the Covenant and read in the hearing of the people. And they said, "All that the LORD has said we will do, and be obedient." And Moses took the blood, sprinkled it on the people, and said, "This is the blood of the covenant which the LORD has made with you according to all these words."

Deuteronomy 5:1-3

And Moses called all Israel, and said to them: "Hear, O Israel, the statutes and judgments which I speak in your hearing today, that you may learn them and be careful to observe them. The LORD our God made a covenant with us in Horeb. The LORD did not make this covenant with our fathers, but with us, those who are here today, all of us who are alive."

This brings us to the next Covenant!

THE COVENANT WITH ISRAEL:

This covenant took place at Sinai, when the people had intimated their acceptance of the Ten Commandments, the very words of the covenant; and they also promised to keep the same. (Exodus 24:3; 34:28)

According to Exodus 23:20-33, it says,

Behold, I send an Angel before you to keep you in the way and to bring you into the place which I have prepared. Beware of Him and obey His voice; do not provoke Him, for He will not pardon your transgressions; for My name is in Him. But if you indeed obey His voice and do all that I speak, then I will be an enemy to your enemies and an adversary to your adversaries. For My Angel will go before you and bring you in to the Amorites and the Hittites and the Perizzites and the Canaanites and the Hivites and the Jebusites; and I will cut them off. You shall not bow down to their gods, nor serve them, nor do according to their works; but you shall utterly overthrow them and completely break down their sacred pillars. "So you shall serve the LORD your God, and He will bless your bread and your water. And I will take sickness away from the midst of you. No one shall suffer miscarriage or be barren in your land; I will fulfill the number of your days. "I will send My fear before you, I will cause confusion among all the people to whom you come, and will make all your enemies turn their backs to you. And I will send hornets before you, which shall drive out the Hivite, the Canaanite, and the Hittite from before you. I will not drive them out from before you in one year, lest the land become desolate and the beasts of the field become too numerous for you. Little by little I will drive them out from before you, until you have increased, and you inherit the land. And I will set your bounds from the Red Sea to the sea, Philistia, and from the desert to the River. For I will deliver the inhabitants of the land into your hand, and you shall drive them out before you. You shall make no covenant with them, nor with their gods. They shall not dwell in your land, lest they make you sin against Me. For if you serve their gods, it will surely be a snare to you."

Their obedience to the commands of the law was to be rewarded by:

• God's constant care of Israel
• Prosperity
• Victory over enemies
• And the pouring out of His Spirit.

The seal of this covenant was the act of circumcision, a procedure unheard of up to this point, but established as the ratification of covenant by the blood that it shed. Genesis 17:9-11, it says,

And God said to Abraham: "As for you, you shall keep My covenant, you and your descendants after you throughout their generations. This is My covenant which you shall keep, between Me and you and your descendants after you: Every male child among you shall be circumcised; and you shall be circumcised in the flesh of your foreskins, and it shall be a sign of the covenant between Me and you."

The Covenant was renewed throughout Jewish history (Deuteronomy Chapter 29; the Book of Joshua; 2 Chronicles 15:1, 23, 29, 34; Ezra 10:3; Nehemiah 9:1-10:39). This brings us to the next Covenant

THE COVENANT WITH DAVID:
This was a more specific covenant than the one made with Abraham. Its main objective was to highlight with greater precision the bloodline through which the blessing promised in the Abrahamic Covenant was to find accomplishment. The royal seed was from then on to be in the house of David as noted in the following: 2 Samuel 7:12 says,

When your days are fulfilled and you rest with your fathers, I will set up your seed after you, who will come from your body, and I will establish his kingdom.

2 Samuel 22:51

He is the tower of salvation to His king, And shows mercy to His anointed, To David and his descendants forevermore.

COVENANT IN THE NEW TESTAMENT:
Jeremiah 31:31-34 says,

"Behold, the days are coming, says the LORD, when I will make a new covenant with the house of Israel and with the house of Judah—not

according to the covenant that I made with their fathers in the day that I took them by the hand to lead them out of the land of Egypt, My covenant which they broke, though I was a husband to them, says the LORD. But this is the covenant that I will make with the house of Israel after those days, says the LORD: I will put My law in their minds, and write it on their hearts; and I will be their God, and they shall be My people. No more shall every man teach his neighbor, and every man his brother, saying, 'Know the LORD,' for they all shall know Me, from the least of them to the greatest of them, says the LORD. For I will forgive their iniquity, and their sin I will remember no more."

Acts 15:20-29

"but that we write to them to abstain from things polluted by idols, from sexual immorality, from things strangled, and from blood. For Moses has had throughout many generations those who preach him in every city, being read in the synagogues every Sabbath." Then it pleased the apostles and elders, with the whole church, to send chosen men of their own company to Antioch with Paul and Barnabas, namely, Judas who was also named Barsabas, and Silas, leading men among the brethren. They wrote this letter by them: The apostles, the elders, and the brethren, To the brethren who are of the Gentiles in Antioch, Syria, and Cilicia: Greetings. Since we have heard that some who went out from us have troubled you with words, unsettling your souls, saying, "You must be circumcised and keep the law"—to whom we gave no such commandment—it seemed good to us, being assembled with one accord, to send chosen men to you with our beloved Barnabas and Paul, men who have risked their lives for the name of our Lord Jesus Christ. We have therefore sent Judas and Silas, who will also report the same things by word of mouth. For it seemed good to the Holy Spirit, and to us, to lay upon you no greater burden than these necessary things: that you abstain from things offered to idols, from blood, from things strangled, and from sexual immorality. If you keep yourselves from these, you will do well. Farewell.

Covenant is like a Kingdom piston that generates the necessary ignition for thrust in the spirit. There is therefore no redemptive initiative from God outside the influence of covenant.

THE END OF THE LAW—OLD TESTAMENT

With the birth of Jesus, we realize that He came to fulfill the Law and to also bring an end to it. We know that Old Covenant came to an end circa AD70 with the complete destruction of the Temple. As a matter of fact, we can say that it actually came to an end the moment Jesus died. This wonderful event is recorded in the Gospel of Matthew 27:51-53, which says,

> *And when Jesus had cried out again in a loud voice, he gave up his spirit. At that moment the curtain of the temple was torn in two from top to bottom. The earth shook and the rocks split. The tombs broke open and the bodies of many holy people who had died were raised to life. They came out of the tombs, and after Jesus' resurrection they went into the holy city and appeared to many people.*

What a world shaking, history-making, show-stopping event was taking place! Jesus Christ had been crucified, had paid the penalty for our sins, and on the third day had risen from the tomb. Matthew reports that the moment Jesus Christ cried out with a loud voice and died that the veil in the Old Covenant Temple was torn from top to bottom [signifying the end to the old system], and that many Old Testament Saints who previously died and were buried, were resurrected. And for three days they remained alive in their tombs. Then, following His resurrection, the graves of many of these Saints were opened and they came into the city. Although the Scriptures do not specify the names of all who were resurrected, I am confident that some of them were mentioned in Hebrews Chapter 11. As a matter this began the great Resurrection, as from that point forward anyone who dies immediately faces the Judgment. There is no longer a holding place for the souls of men when they die as was the case pre Jesus' death, burial and His Resurrection. Jesus became the new and living way into the Father's Presence and as such made a way for all who would now trust and obey Him. All others will face God's eternal judgment and separation from Him.

THE BIRTH OF THE NEW TESTAMENT

So with the death, burial and resurrection of Jesus Christ we saw the end of the Old Covenant system and the arrival of the New Covenant. This Covenant was now established between Jesus and His new Bride, the Church. All the rituals were now over and the pomp and splendour of the Old Covenant Temple was over. God removed His Presence from the former brick and mortar Temple made with men's hands to the spiritual New Covenant Temple [the lives of those who accepted Him as Lord and Saviour]. This new Temple [the Church] was going to be His permanent home.

THE NEW TESTAMENT REVEALED

Solomon's temple was the first to be glorified. It prophesied of the greater Temple that was to come. This greater Temple is not a physical temple, but rather the one that Paul described in Ephesians 2:20-22, which says,

> *Having been built upon the foundation of the apostles and prophets, Christ Jesus Himself being the corner stone, in whom the whole building, being fitted together is growing into a holy temple in the Lord; in whom you also are being built together into a dwelling of God in the Spirit.* NASB

Apostle Paul was speaking of the corporate Temple made up of the entire Body of Christ. Peter says of this Temple, that we are "living stones" 1 Peter 2:5, used to build it. There is another sense in which, we as individuals, are also a complete Temple in ourselves, for Paul in 1 Corinthians 3:16 says,

> *Do you not know that you are a temple of God, and that the Spirit of God dwells in you?* NASB

In this individual sense, we can make the comparison of the three parts of the Temple with the three parts of our being. The Temple consisted of an outer court, the holy place, and the Most Holy Place. Our personal "temples" contain body, soul, and spirit.

The point is to show that in the Old Testament God dwelt in buildings made of wood and stone, but that these were never intended to be the final dwelling place of God. Even Solomon recognized this as recorded in 1 Kings 8:27, which says,

> *But will God indeed dwell on the earth? Behold, heaven and the highest heaven cannot contain Thee, how much less this house, which I have built!* NASB

Solomon recognized the impossibility of building an earthly house that could house the glory of God. And so he hinted of a greater Temple that was yet to come, one made of living stones and Holy Spirit callings and ministries ("vessels" and "pillars").

In this new Temple would also be a new order of priests, not of Levi but of Melchizedek. The priests of Levi were a temporary order of priests, called to minister during the time of the Old Covenant. One had to be descended from Aaron to minister in that temple. But in the New Covenant Order, the Melchizedek priests did not have to be descended from Aaron, but from Jesus Christ, not in a natural manner but as spiritual Sons of God.

The Melchizedek priesthood was older than that of Levi. The original king of Salem (Jerusalem) was not of Levi, because he came long before Levi was even born. Years later, David was a priest of the Melchizedek Order, even though he himself was not a Levite Psalms 110:4 says,

> *The Lord has sworn and will not change His mind, Thou art a priest forever according to the order of Melchizedek.* NASB

David was of the tribe of Judah, and so he was not eligible to be a Levitical priest, as they had to be of the tribe of Levi. Instead, like the original Melchizedek, he ruled Jerusalem, the "city of Salem." But in the greater sense, all of this prophesied of the New Jerusalem, which would be ruled by David's greater Son, King Jesus.

Jesus Christ was of the tribe of Judah, and so it was not lawful for Him to be High Priest of the order of Levi. He came as High Priest of Melchizedek. Hebrews 7:11-14 says:

> *Now if perfection was through the Levitical priesthood [for on the basis of it the people received the Law], what further need was there*

for another priest to arise according to the order of Melchizedek, and not be designated according to the order of Aaron? For when the priesthood is changed, of necessity there takes place a change of law also. For the One concerning whom these things are spoken belongs to another tribe, from which no one has officiated at the altar. For it is evident that our Lord was descended from Judah, a tribe with reference to which Moses spoke nothing concerning priests. NASB

Jesus Christ is the High Priest of an entirely new order of priests, whose sacrifice is the Lamb of God alone. Neither the High Priest nor his children, as the sons of God, are eligible by law to offer animal sacrifices, nor are these effective after the Cross.

Jesus is not going to return to the old Jerusalem to be High Priest over Levitical priests making animal sacrifices in a physical temple; no, He is already the High Priest of a New Temple: The Church and High Priest of the New Covenant. The New Covenant is not a temporary interlude after which time the Old Covenant provisions will be reinstated. The Old Covenant was faulty and has become obsolete. The "better" Covenant and its provisions are here to stay. The Bible says that those who promote the old way do not know the mind of Christ. Hebrews 8:13 says,

When He said, "A New Covenant," He has made the first obsolete. But whatever is becoming obsolete and growing old is ready to disappear. NASB

The New Covenant, on the other hand, will never grow old, nor will it ever become obsolete. The New Covenant is known as an Everlasting Covenant, and something that is everlasting is just that everlasting; not having any end!

The Book of Acts and The Arrival of The Holy Spirit—Beginning of The New Covenant

This was the command of Jesus to His early Apostles: Acts 1:1-8 says,

The former account I made, O Theophilus, of all that Jesus began both to do and teach, until the day in which He was taken up, after He through the Holy Spirit had given commandments to the

apostles whom He had chosen, to whom He also presented Himself alive after His suffering by many infallible proofs, being seen by them during forty days and speaking of the things pertaining to the kingdom of God. And being assembled together with them, He commanded them not to depart from Jerusalem, but to wait for the Promise of the Father, "which," He said, "you have heard from Me; for John truly baptized with water, but you shall be baptized with the Holy Spirit not many days from now." Therefore, when they had come together, they asked Him, saying, "Lord, will You at this time restore the kingdom to Israel?" And He said to them, "It is not for you to know times or seasons which the Father has put in His own authority. But you shall receive power when the Holy Spirit has come upon you; and you shall be witnesses to Me in Jerusalem, and in all Judea and Samaria, and to the end of the earth."

We know that this occurred not long after He was taken up to Heaven as recorded in the following Verses: Acts 2:1-4, 14-47 says,

When the Day of Pentecost had fully come, they were all with one accord in one place. And suddenly there came a sound from heaven, as of a rushing mighty wind, and it filled the whole house where they were sitting. Then there appeared to them divided tongues, as of fire, and one sat upon each of them. And they were all filled with the Holy Spirit and began to speak with other tongues, as the Spirit gave them utterance."... But Peter, standing up with the eleven, raised his voice and said to them, "Men of Judea and all who dwell in Jerusalem, let this be known to you, and heed my words. For these are not drunk, as you suppose, since it is only the third hour of the day. But this is what was spoken by the prophet Joel: 'And it shall come to pass in the last days, says God, That I will pour out of My Spirit on all flesh; Your sons and your daughters shall prophesy, Your young men shall see visions, Your old men shall dream dreams. And on My menservants and on My maidservants I will pour out My Spirit in those days; And they shall prophesy. I will show wonders in heaven above And signs in the earth beneath: Blood and fire and vapour of smoke. The sun shall be turned into darkness, And the moon into blood, Before the coming of the great and awesome day of the LORD. And it shall come to pass That whoever calls on the name of the LORD Shall be saved.' "Men of Israel, hear these words: Jesus of Nazareth, a Man attested by God to you by miracles, wonders, and signs which God did through Him in your midst, as you yourselves also know—Him, being delivered by the determined purpose and foreknowledge of God, you have taken by lawless hands, have crucified, and put to death; whom God raised up, having loosed the pains of death, because it was not possible that He should be held by it. For David says concerning Him: 'I foresaw the LORD always before my face, For He is at my right hand, that I may not be shaken. Therefore my heart rejoiced, and my tongue was glad; Moreover my flesh also will rest in hope. For You will not leave my soul in Hades, Nor will You allow Your Holy One to see corruption. You have made known to me the ways of life; You will make me full of joy in Your presence.' "Men and brethren, let me speak freely to you of the patriarch David, that he is both dead and buried, and his tomb is with us to this day. Therefore, being a prophet, and knowing that God had sworn with an oath to him that of the fruit of his body, according to the flesh, He would raise up the Christ to sit on his throne, he, foreseeing this, spoke concerning the resurrection of the Christ, that His soul was not left in Hades, nor did His flesh see corruption. This Jesus God has raised up, of which we are all witnesses. Therefore being exalted to the right hand of God, and having received from the Father the promise of the Holy Spirit, He poured out this which you now see and hear. "For David did not ascend into the heavens, but he says himself: 'The LORD said to my Lord, "Sit at My right hand, Till I make Your enemies Your footstool."' "Therefore let all the house of Israel know assuredly that God has made this Jesus, whom you crucified, both Lord and Christ." Now when they heard this, they were cut to the heart, and said to Peter and the rest of the apostles, "Men and brethren, what shall we do?" Then Peter said to them, "Repent, and let every one of you be baptized in the name of Jesus Christ for the remission of sins; and you shall receive the gift of the Holy Spirit. For the promise is to you and to your children, and to all who are afar off, as many as the Lord our God will call." And with many other words he testified and exhorted them, saying, "Be saved from this perverse generation."

Then those who gladly received his word were baptized; and that day about three thousand souls were added to them. And they continued steadfastly in the apostles' doctrine and fellowship, in the breaking of bread, and in prayers. Then fear came upon every soul, and many wonders and signs were done through the apostles. Now all who believed were together, and had all things in common, and sold their possessions and goods, and divided them among all, as anyone had need. So continuing daily with one accord in the temple, and breaking bread from house to house, they ate their food with gladness and simplicity of heart, praising God and having favour with all the people. And the Lord added to the church daily those who were being saved.

The Church then became and continues to be the New Israel of God. We saw the prototype [physical Israel] reign come to an end. And remember that the Church is eternal and has no end. There is never, ever going to be another covenant as the one Jesus Christ has made is the eternal one. His blood is the answer to our dilemma and it is sufficient!

In our next chapter we would explore some of the author's Ponderings on the Many Comings of Jesus. The following chapter is from Dr. John Noë's book titled "The Greater Jesus", which can be purchased through Amazon, and used by permission.

CHAPTER EIGHT
MY PONDERINGS ON THE MANY COMINGS OF JESUS

IN THIS CHAPTER I WOULD LIKE TO BORROW A TEACHING BY DR. JOHN NOË THAT I find to be of great significance and importance to the Body of Christ. Dr. John Noë writes with depth, clarity and wisdom that is so much needed in the earth today. This teaching is from his book titled "The Greater Jesus", which I highly recommend, especially for those who take Bible study very seriously.

FIVE EMPHATIC TIME STATEMENTS OF JESUS
Before we get into the "many" comings of Jesus allow me to share this first. I would like for us to look at these Five Emphatic Time Statements of Jesus [*spoken almost 2000 years ago*]...

As we study these five time statements, please honestly and sincerely ask yourself how would you have understood these words of Jesus if you had been with Him back then and there, sitting at His feet, and listening, intently?

Matthew 10:23 While talking with His disciples, Jesus promised.

When they persecute you in this city, flee to another. For assuredly, I say to you, you will not have gone through the cities of Israel before the Son of Man comes.

Matthew 16:27-28 He informed His disciples.

For the Son of Man will come in the glory of His Father with His angels, and then He will reward each according to his works. Assuredly, I say to you, there are some standing here who shall not taste death till they see the Son of Man coming in His kingdom.

Matthew 26:64 Quoting from the prophet Daniel, Jesus responded to and forewarned Caiaphas, the high priest, and the Sanhedrin saying.

Jesus said to him, "It is as you said. Nevertheless, I say to you, hereafter you will see the Son of Man sitting at the right hand of the Power, and coming on the clouds of heaven."

Matthew 24:3, 27, 30, 34 Jesus divinely linked the time of His coming to the destruction of the Temple.

Now as He sat on the Mount of Olives, the disciples came to Him privately, saying, "Tell us, when will these things be? And what will be the sign of Your coming, and of the end of the age?"

For as the lightning comes from the east and flashes to the west, so also will the coming of the Son of Man be.

Then the sign of the Son of Man will appear in heaven, and then all the tribes of the earth will mourn, and they will see the Son of Man coming on the clouds of heaven with power and great glory.

Assuredly, I say to you, this generation will by no means pass away till all these things take place.

John 21:22 When Peter asked about John.

Jesus said to him, "If I will that he remain till I come, what is that to you? You follow Me."

For centuries, theologians have tried every way imaginable to get around these "embarrassing," time-restrictive statements of Jesus, while at the same time recognizing that Jesus' first followers understood Jesus' words in a plain, simple, and natural way as applying to them, there and then.

So the question becomes—how would you have understood these words if you were living and learning them straight from Jesus back then, almost two thousand years ago?

Here is another point or reason for the 1ˢᵗ Century Believers' air of expectancy and relevancy. This is one that I think you will find equally compelling.

According to the Bible, Jesus' first followers, including the inspired writers of the New Testament books, were guided into all truth and told the things that were yet to come by the Holy Spirit (John 16:13 for reference *"However, when He, the Spirit of truth, has come, He will guide you into all truth; for He will not speak on His own authority, but whatever He hears He will speak; and He will tell you things to come."*). Obviously, their expectations were formed by this divine guidance.

But here is the rub, however. If their Holy-Spirit-guided expectations for Jesus coming on the clouds and fulfilling "**_all things_**" within their lifetime have been proven false by nineteen centuries and counting, how can we trust them to have conveyed other aspects of the faith along to us accurately—such as the requirements for salvation, etc.?

Three other factors worth serious reconsideration are these:

1.   If Amos 3:7 is true—that God *"does nothing without revealing His plan to His servants the prophets"*—then why didn't at least one Holy-Spirit-guided, New Testament writer ever correct these 1st-century-fulfillment expectations?
The fact is, none did. Nor did they ever re-explain or contradict Jesus' teachings regarding the timeframe for His coming in judgement—i.e., "**this [that] generation.**"
2.   God does not lie (Hebrews 6:18; Titus 1:2)
3.   He created time and does not purposely mislead or speak to us in words we cannot properly understand. Theologians term this divine attribute the perspicuity of Scripture, meaning clearness and ease in being understood.

Instead, the New Testament writers did the exact opposite. At Jesus' literal forty-year, "**_this [that] generation_**" time period wound down, from AD 30 through AD 70, the sense of nearness language in the New Testament dramatically picked up. I call this "the intensification of nearness language."

This intensification provides further proof that Jesus' first followers understood His words to come on the clouds and fulfil "**all things**" as applying to them, then and there.

However, before we go into this **Intensification of Nearness Language** allow me to say this, or answer the following question:

Why Jesus' Birth Is Never Called His 'First Coming'

Now understand this… For there to be a so-called "Second Coming" there must first be a "First Coming"…

Have you ever wondered why Jesus' birth (around 4 B.C.) is never called His "first coming" in Scripture? It's for a good reason—it wasn't.

It was simply stated in Matthew 1:22-23; Luke 1:30-33; John 1:14… It was as if Jesus just simply manifested in time and space and we beheld Him.

> So all this was done that it might be fulfilled which was spoken by the Lord through the prophet, saying: "Behold, the virgin shall be with child, and bear a Son, and they shall call His name Immanuel," which is translated, "God with us."

> Then the angel said to her, "Do not be afraid, Mary, for you have found favour with God. And behold, you will conceive in your womb and bring forth a Son, and shall call His name JESUS. He will be great, and will be called the Son of the Highest; and the Lord God will give Him the throne of His father David. And He will reign over the house of Jacob forever, and of His kingdom there will be no end."

> And the Word became flesh and dwelt among us, and we beheld His glory, the glory as of the only begotten of the Father, full of grace and truth.

This misconception only leads to the improper numbering of another coming as His "second coming"—which it isn't either.

The whole idea that Jesus is off somewhere waiting to return to planet Earth at some future time is just as erroneous, biblically, as the notion of limiting His comings to only two, three, or to any at all.

Again, it's the classic case of the traditions of men that *"nullify the word of God"* or make it of *"none effect"* (Mark 7:13; Matthew 15:6 – NIV/ KJV).

Hear me: God's Word clearly documents and teaches that the comings (plural) of Jesus run like a thread throughout both the Old and New Testaments, which we shall deal with later on...

Usually, Jesus came to individuals; He came suddenly, unexpectedly, and unannounced; He came to bring aid, to judge, to assign a task, or to proclaim a message.

Often His coming and appearing was recognized only by the person for whom it was intended.

These comings produced profound, life-altering impacts upon those who received them, and in turn upon other people and nations who were touched by that person's subsequent life and ministry.

INTENSIFICATION OF NEARNESS LANGUAGE

Approximately nineteen years after Jesus delivered His most dramatic prophecy in what is termed His Olivet Discourse (Matthew 24, Mark 13, Luke 21), the writers of the New Testament began writing their epistles, or what we now call the books of the New Testament. The intensification of their nearness language is most evident.

To dramatize it, I will provide a recap and countdown by using "**T minus**" the number of years remaining in Jesus' forty-year, **this generation time period**, along with the approximate dates when these works were written.

Once again, before we go any further, ask yourself how would you have understood their intensifying words if you had been living back then, almost 2000 years ago?

"T minus 40 years" (circa AD 30)—*Jesus said*—"I tell you the truth, this generation will certainly not pass away until all these things have happened" (Matthew 24:34).

According to Deuteronomy 18:22,

If what a prophet proclaims in the name of the Lord does not take place or come true, that is a message the Lord has not spoken. Do not be afraid of him.

If Jesus was a true prophet, *what* He said would happen must happen, but also it must happen *when* He said that it would.

"T minus 21 years" (circa AD 49)—Paul wrote—*"The fullness of time was come"* (Galatians 4:4).

What "fullness" of what "time" was Paul talking about nineteen years after Jesus' earthly ministry? If back then was the "fullness," does time ever get **more full?**

"T minus 13 years" (circa AD 57)—Paul wrote—*"Time is short"* (1 Corinthians 7:29)... *"The world in its present form is passing away"* (1 Corinthians 7:31).

We hear this first statement a lot nowadays. But whose time was short and what world was passing away back then?

"T minus 12 years" (circa AD 58)—Paul wrote—*"Understand the present time.... because our salvation is nearer now that when we first believed. The night is nearly over, the day is almost here"* (Romans 13:11-12).

Paul and some of these Romans first believed twenty to thirty years earlier. Now only twelve years remained until the end of Jesus' literal, forty-year, "this generation" time period.

Something truly significant was about to happen.

It doesn't take a modern-day rocket scientist or a high-speed computer to do this simple math.

"T minus 12 years" (circa AD 58)—Paul wrote—*"The God of peace will soon [shortly] crush Satan under your feet"* (Romans 16:20).

Here is an unmistakable reference to the nearness of a day of deliverance for Christians who were being persecuted by enemies that surrounded them.

"T minus 10 years" (circa AD 60)—*James wrote*—*"be patient and stand firm, because the Lord's coming is near (at hand).... The judge is standing at the door!"* (James 5:8-9).

James' words are some of the strongest in the Bible indicating the nearness of Jesus' coming in judgement. Jesus had told His disciples in His Olivet Discourse that **"So you also, when you see all these things, know that it [He] is near—at the door"** (Matthew 24:33), and not nineteen hundred plus years away.

Now, with only ten years left in Jesus' forty-year countdown, James writes to real, living, air-breathing, and blood-pumping human beings and admonishes them to have patience as a present-relevant virtue, not a futuristic deception. And here are unmistakable indications of the nearness of this event, and not just mere expressions of hope.

"**T minus 5 years**" (circa AD 65)—The writer of Hebrews wrote—*"but in these last days he [God] has spoken to us by his Son… . (Hebrews 1:2).*

Please, please understand this: By divine inspiration, the writer of Hebrews affixes two specific historical events to the biblical time period know as the "**last days**":

1. The time of Jesus' earthly ministry and
2. The time in which he was writing.

Clearly, he saw himself living in the "**last days**," back then and there.

The question then becomes: those were the "last days" of what? As we have seen, they were the "last days" of the biggest thing that was ending at the time or ever will end on planet Earth and in redemptive and world history.

"**T minius 5 years**" (circa AD 65)—The writer of Hebrews wrote—*"In just a very little while, 'He who is coming will come and will not delay'"… . (Hebrews 10:37).*

In direct contradiction of this verse, the Church has been preaching delay for nineteen centuries and counting. The question is, who is right—the inspired writer of Hebrews or the uninspired Church and its modern-day prophecy-postponement experts.

Also, when we compare this "**little while**" phrase with Jesus' seven uses of "a little while" in John 16:16-19, we see that Jesus' "a little while" was only a matter of a week or two before He was arrested, tried, and crucified.

A $^{(1)}$little while, and you will not see Me; and again $^{(2)}$a little while, and you will see Me, because I go to the Father." Then some of His disciples said among themselves, "What is this that He says to us, '$^{(3)}$A little while, and you will not see Me; and again $^{(4)}$a little while, and you will see Me'; and, 'because I go to the Father'?" They said therefore, "What is this that He says, '$^{(5)}$A little while'? We do not know what He is saying." Now Jesus knew that they desired to ask

Him, and He said to them, "Are you inquiring among yourselves about what I said, ⁽⁶⁾A little while, and you will not see Me; and again ⁽⁷⁾a little while, and you will see Me'? [Parenthesis mine]

The entire book of Hebrews conveys this same sense of nearness. For example, "**as you see the Day approaching**" (Hebrews 10:25). This and other statements like it, cannot be ignored, twisted, or lightly brushed aside.

When Hebrews was written, the early Church was undergoing intense persecution from the Jews and the Roman Emperor Nero. These Believers were eagerly awaiting Jesus' promised coming in judgement.

Again, ask yourself, how could they "see the Day approaching" if this Day was two millennia in the future?

Let's also note that Jesus said it was the "evil servant" who says "My Lord delayeth his coming" (Matthew 24:48 *KJV*).

"T minus 3-5 years" (circa AD 65-67)—Peter wrote —*"The end of all things is at hand."* (1 Peter 4:7 KJV).

Peter's words are not "the end of some things" or "the middle of all things," but *"the end of all things." "***At hand***"* is the Greek word *engys.* It is the ultimate nearness idiom and means "graspable, seizible, there for the taking, or almost there."

For Example:

- John the Baptist proclaimed, "the kingdom of heaven is at hand," referring to the nearness of Jesus' earthly ministry (Matthew 3:2). His ministry began within months.
- Jesus used it when He said, "behold the hour is at hand" for his betrayal by Judas (Matthew 26:45 KJV), and *"behold, he is at hand that doth betray me"* (Matthew 26:46 KJV).
- Jesus also proclaimed *"the Kingdom of God is at hand"* (Mark 1:15) and sent His disciples out to proclaim and minister the same *"at hand"* kingdom (Matthew 10:7).
- The Apostle John used it when He said the Jewish Passover was *"at hand"*—meaning, *"almost time"* (John 11:55).
- Paul wrote to Timothy, *"the time of my departure is at hand"* (2 Timothy 4:6).

All of them were saying that those events would be soon—certainly within their lifetime or generation…

Neither Pater's nor James' hearers and readers understood or interpreted their "**at hand**" time terminology as meaning 2,000 years-or-a-longer period, as many of us have been taught today.

Neither was Peter nor James deceiving their audience with a different or specialized meaning of known and ordinary words. They issued no disclaimers. Their "**at hand**" demands the same "right there" or "almost right there" immediacy as its use in other New Testament Scriptures, including the Book of Revelation.

"**At hand**" means "**there**" or "**real soon**," and not centuries later.

However, let us not forget that when we read these words of Peter we are reading someone else's mail. Peter's 1st century letter was addressed "To God's elect, strangers in the world, scattered throughout Pontus, Galatia, Cappadocia, Asia and Bithynia" (1 Peter 1:1).

He wasn't writing to them about Christians living in the 21st Century. That again, is taking his words totally out of context. Basic interpretative principles demand audience relevancy. Either "the end of all things" Peter was talking about came upon them back then and there or Peter was mistaken and uninspired. Plain and Simple…

Furthermore, while Peter was saying "**the end of all things is at hand,**" scoffers present back then (Jude 17-19) were saying, "*Where is this 'coming' He promised? Ever since our fathers died, everything goes on as it has…*" (2 Peter 3:4).

So, who has history proven was right? The 1st Century scoffers or Apostle Peter?

Indeed, something catastrophic was impending, there and then—almost 2,000 years ago. Ten verses later Peter explains:

"**T minus 3-5 years**" (circa AD 65-67)—Peter wrote —"*For it is time for judgement to begin with the family [the house] of God…*" (1 Peter 4:17 KJV).

Peter, like Jesus, was emphatic. He did not say it "might be" or "someday will be." He said, "For it is time!"

A catastrophe was imminent! The time for judgement was to begin at the House of God. There is no other legitimate explanation. Peter further revealed that Jesus was also "ready to judge the living and the dead" (1 Peter 4:5).

What had once been seen afar off by the ancient prophets was now ready to be revealed to Peter's "you" group in the "last time" [almost 2,000 years ago] (1 Peter 1:5, 12 see also Acts 3:24).

"T minus 2-3 years" (circa AD 67-68)—John wrote—*"Little children, this is the last hour... it is the last hour" (1 John 2:18).*

Twice in this one verse John says this. Written on the eve of the destruction of Jerusalem and the Temple, John, like Peter, does not say **"might be"** or **"someday will be"** but "*it is/[was] the last hour*."

Tell me when you go through the Holy Scriptures with this level of careful study, then who can deny it?

Please, I believe that we have more than enough Scriptural evidence that warrants us fully believing that much of what we have been taught all or most of our Christian lives have been false.

That we need to take the Scriptures in the light of who it was intended for and that was the FIRST CENTURY BELIEVERS. And as such we MUST read and study the Scriptures from a 1st century context and understanding. Hence the reason that Audience Relevance is vital.

And while your misunderstanding of this vital aspect of the Scriptures will not prevent you from entering heaven, it will surely limit and significantly restrict your power and ability to function and triumphantly navigate God's Kingdom advance upon planet Earth...

I truly believe that we are in time of increased revelation as Apostles continue to press into Father and into His Word.

Fresh 'new/old' truths are being proclaimed that have significant relevance on how we function in this life. We need these truths and we need to be truly Bible-believing Saints, not those who just run with the latest 'futurist' fad but deal with things in their context...

Some fifty-some years ago, some Christians who believed that "Jesus was coming again soon" began purchasing wall plaques reading— "PERHAPS TODAY!"

Today, they claim "the signs described in the Bible," which were so obvious 50 years ago, have only grown in intensity and "are coming to pass at a rapid rate."

Surely, the Lord's Second Coming is not only soon and getting sooner, they surmise, but we are living in "Earth's Final Moments ... as we look forward to Jesus' return."

And even though the nineteen-centuries-and-counting trail of speculative and failed predictions has had a profoundly negative effect upon the Church and upon the credibility of Christianity as a whole, this non occurrence factor is ignored in favour of now being the right time.

First, I believe every word the Bible says about the coming of the Lord—but not what most tradition-bound preachers say about it.

Secondly, and in the words of the Nicene Creed, "I believe ... He [Jesus] shall come again with glory to judge both the living and the dead; Whose kingdom shall have no end."

Let's do a groundbreaking exercise before we go further in this teaching: I ask: How would you answer the following?

QUESTION:

IN YOUR OPINION ... OVER THE ENTIRE COURSE OF HUMAN HISTORY—PAST, PRESENT AND FUTURE—HOW MANY COMINGS OF JESUS ARE THERE?

ANSWERS:

A) ONE?

B) TWO?

C) THREE?

D) FOUR?

E) MORE?

After all, the Bible does tell us to "test" and to "prove all things" (1 Thessalonians 5:21). The coming of Jesus is certainly part of "all things."

What answer did you pick?

Most people pick "B) Two," because nothing has been more strongly emphasized throughout Church history than the so-called, "Second Coming" of Jesus Christ and its implied limitation of only two comings.

But the biblically correct answer is "E) More."

Yes, you may be amazed—I was when I first discovered it—at how little knowledge most of us have about the Bible and the Christian faith in this fundamental area.

Consequently, I want to begin to move you onward and upward from waiting only for the Second Coming to begin to see, through God's Word, the full and glorious reality of Jesus' many comings (plural).

Hopefully, this will clear up many misconceptions and open the way for us, as Christians, to unite and stop limiting His comings to merely a past event or a future hope! Of course, it's not what I or any other human being says about the coming of Jesus that counts, but what the Word of God says about it.

Neither the Second Coming nor Return of Christ Fits the Terminology of Scripture Popular TV Evangelists, Bible Teachers, and Church Pastors commonly claim that the Bible speaks extensively about the Second Coming of Christ, mentioning it many times in the New Testament.

A famous world renowned Evangelist, in one of his crusades and in a January 2004 article in his very popular magazine titled, "The End of the World," claimed, "the Bible speaks extensively about the Second Coming of Christ, mentioning it more than 300 times in the New Testament. By comparison, repentance ... is mentioned about 70 times, and baptism ... is mentioned about 20 times." He concluded, "It is obvious, then, that the Holy Spirit, who inspired the Scriptures, places great importance on the return of Jesus Christ."

With all due respect for this world-renowned Evangelist, do you know what the Bible actually says (literally mentions) about a "Second Coming?" Nothing!

Nowhere does the Bible use the term Second Coming. It's a non-biblical term. Nor does the Bible use the term Return in direct association with Jesus.

Factually, the Bible contains many references to many different comings of Jesus, but none to a single "Second Coming."

Please be assured that by pointing out this biblical fact, I am not intending to diminish, detract from, or mock the "promise of His coming" in any way. Rather, I'm justifying why the doctrine of a "Second Coming" and "Return" must be faced anew.

Most everyone recognizes that words matter, and wording is important. With this in mind, "The words 'return' and 'second coming' are not properly speaking Biblical words in that the two words do not represent any equivalent Greek words." This is a major admission with huge implications.

Another fact is, we Christians have been hamstrung for centuries with these two non-scriptural expressions and unscriptural mindsets.

As we shall soon discover, biblically, the idea that Jesus is off somewhere waiting to come back at some future time, as well as the idea of limiting the comings of Jesus to only two or three times, or to any at all, is man's idea and not God's.

The closest we can come to the phraseology of a "Second Coming" is in Hebrews 9:28, which says,

So Christ was sacrificed once to take away the sins of many people; and he will appear a second time, not to bear sin, but to bring salvation to those who are waiting for him.

Contrary to popular belief, this Scripture does not limit, number, or confine Jesus' comings to only two times.

Rather, it highlights two specific and significant comings, among many—see a partial list in 1 Corinthians 15:5-8 for instance—and for a special salvation-fulfilment purpose.

For I delivered to you first of all that which I also received: that Christ died for our sins according to the Scriptures, and that He was buried, and that He rose again the third day according to the Scriptures, and that He was seen by Cephas, then by the twelve. After that He was seen by over five hundred brethren at once, of whom the greater part remain to the present, but some have fallen asleep. After that He was seen by James, then by all the apostles. Then last of all He was seen by me also, as by one born out of due time.

This "second-time" coming follows the typology of Israel's high priest on the Day of Atonement, which occurred every year.

And please remember that Christ as both our sacrifice and our High Priest (see Hebrews 7:27-28; 9:11-15) had to come and fulfil this typology, perfectly (also see Hebrews chapters 8, 9, and 10).

who does not need daily, as those high priests, to offer up sacrifices, first for His own sins and then for the people's, for this He did once for all when He offered up Himself. For the law appoints as high priests men who have weakness, but the word of the oath, which came after the law, appoints the Son who has been perfected forever.

But Christ came as High Priest of the good things to come, with the greater and more perfect tabernacle not made with hands, that is, not of this creation. Not with the blood of goats and calves, but with His own blood He entered the Most Holy Place once for all, having obtained eternal redemption. For if the blood of bulls and goats and the ashes of a heifer, sprinkling the unclean, sanctifies for the purifying of the flesh, how much more shall the blood of Christ, who through the eternal Spirit offered Himself without spot to God, cleanse your conscience from dead works to serve the living God? And for this reason He is the Mediator of the new covenant, by means of death, for the redemption of the transgressions under the first covenant, that those who are called may receive the promise of the eternal inheritance.

Far-fetched? Think about it! If we persist in limiting the comings of Jesus to only two times and in calling the babe in the manger the "first coming" of Jesus, as so many do, that means the "Second Coming" is over.

- Chronologically, the 'second coming' happened after Jesus was crucified and ascended to heaven, when He came and appeared to Stephen during his trial before the Jewish Sanhedrin (Acts 7:55-56).

But he, being full of the Holy Spirit, gazed into heaven and saw the glory of God, and Jesus standing at the right hand of God, and said, "Look! I see the heavens opened and the Son of Man standing at the right hand of God!"

- Or it happened when Jesus came and appeared to Saul on the road to Damascus (Acts 9:1-8),

Then Saul, still breathing threats and murder against the disciples of the Lord, went to the high priest and asked letters from him to the synagogues of Damascus, so that if he found any who were of the Way, whether men or women, he might bring them bound to Jerusalem. As he journeyed he came near Damascus, and suddenly a light shone around him from heaven. Then he fell to the ground, and heard a voice saying to him, "Saul, Saul, why are you persecuting Me?" And he said, "Who are You, Lord?" Then the Lord said, "I am Jesus, whom you are persecuting. It is hard for you to kick against the goads." So he, trembling and astonished, said, "Lord, what do You want me to do?" Then the Lord said to him, "Arise and go into the city, and you will be told what you must do." And the men who journeyed with him stood speechless, hearing a voice but seeing no one. Then Saul arose from the ground, and when his eyes were opened he saw no one. But they led him by the hand and brought him into Damascus.

• Or to John in the Revelation (Revelation 1 and John 21:22-23).

I, John, both your brother and companion in the tribulation and kingdom and patience of Jesus Christ, was on the island that is called Patmos for the word of God and for the testimony of Jesus Christ. I was in the Spirit on the Lord's Day, and I heard behind me a loud voice, as of a trumpet, saying, "I am the Alpha and the Omega, the First and the Last," and, "What you see, write in a book and send it to the seven churches which are in Asia: to Ephesus, to Smyrna, to Pergamos, to Thyatira, to Sardis, to Philadelphia, and to Laodicea." Then I turned to see the voice that spoke with me. And having turned I saw seven golden lampstands, and in the midst of the seven lampstands One like the Son of Man, clothed with a garment down to the feet and girded about the chest with a golden band. His head and hair were white like wool, as white as snow, and His eyes like a flame of fire; His feet were like fine brass, as if refined in a furnace, and His voice as the sound of many waters; He had in His right hand seven stars, out of His mouth went a sharp two-edged sword, and His countenance was like the sun shining in its strength. And when I saw Him, I fell at His feet as dead. But He laid His right hand on me, saying to me, "Do not be afraid; I am the First and the Last. I am He who lives, and was dead, and behold, I am alive forevermore. Amen. And I have the keys of Hades and of Death."

Jesus said to him, "If I will that he remain till I come, what is that to you? You follow Me." Then this saying went out among the brethren that this disciple would not die. Yet Jesus did not say to him that he would not die, but, "If I will that he remain till I come, what is that to you?"

How do you count or discount those comings of Jesus? And, as we shall see shortly, there are many more comings of Jesus.

At this point, you may be feeling a bit perplexed by my last few statements. Or, you may be upset. But before you react in a knee-jerk fashion (again, I know how emotional this can be), let's define what we mean by "a coming of Jesus." Then we'll consider the biblical evidence.

Please don't dismiss any of this too quickly, and until you've considered it all.

My working definition for "a coming of Jesus" is this: it's a personal and bodily intervention and/or manifestation of Jesus into the life of an individual, a group, a church, or a nation on this earth.

As we shall see, there are many different types of comings for different purposes, and they occur at different times and places. Some are visible appearances; some are invisible interventions.

He Never Left

While God's Word clearly documents and teaches that the comings (plural) of Jesus run like a thread throughout both the Old and New Testaments, the word "return" is also never used.

Like the expression "Second Coming," it is non-scriptural terminology, an unscriptural concept, and a non-event.

To this point, I submit that authentic Christianity does not stand for a departed and absent Christ—absent the entire length of the Christian age!

Ironically, it stands for a departed but still present and active Christ who never left and has truly, wholly, and totally been with his Church and people for over nineteen centuries and is still with us today. How do I know He never left? He told us so.

Of course, at one point early in His earthly ministry, Jesus also told His disciples that a time would come when He would be "taken from them" (Mark 2:20).

Then later, toward the end of his ministry, Jesus said He was "going there [heaven] to prepare a place for you." And, He promised to "come again" to "take you to be with me that you also may be where I am." (John 14:2-4).

He said his going away (John 16:5, 16) was required and the decisive factor for the coming of the Holy Spirit (John 16:7).

But also, in what may seem to be a contradiction, He told them that "I will not leave you as orphans" (John 14:18).

And then, at the end of His famous Great Commission in Matthew 28:18-20, He also assured His 1st-Century followers that He would be with them, "And surely I will be with you always, to [until] the very end of the age" Matthew 28:20b

In a similar manner, Jesus previously had promised, "For where two or three come together in my name, there am I with them" Matthew 18:20

So how can Jesus go somewhere, i.e., depart, and still be with them? Can these two seemingly paradoxical notions be reconciled?

The traditional explanation has been that what Jesus was really saying was He would be with them in the future in the Person of the Holy Spirit, Whom He was to send at Pentecost (Acts 2).

The verse, "the Lord is the Spirit," is cited in support (2 Corinthians 3:17). But the outpouring of the Holy Spirit was a separately and distinctly prophesied event from the Old Testament (see Ezekiel 36:26-27; 37:9-14; 39:29; Joel 2:28-32) and a singular happening in the New Testament (see Acts 2).

Ezekiel 36:26-27 says,

I will give you a new heart and put a new spirit within you; I will take the heart of stone out of your flesh and give you a heart of flesh. I will put My Spirit within you and cause you to walk in My statutes, and you will keep My judgments and do them.

Ezekiel 37:9-14

Also He said to me, "Prophesy to the breath, prophesy, son of man, and say to the breath, 'Thus says the Lord GOD: "Come from the four winds, O breath, and breathe on these slain, that they may live."" So I prophesied as He commanded me, and breath came into them, and they lived, and stood upon their feet, an exceedingly great army. Then He said to me, "Son of man, these bones are the whole house of Israel. They indeed say, 'Our bones are dry, our hope is lost, and we ourselves are cut off!' Therefore prophesy and say to them, 'Thus says the Lord GOD: "Behold, O My people, I will open your graves and cause you to come up from your graves, and bring you into the land of Israel. Then you shall know that I am the LORD, when I have opened your graves, O My people, and brought you up from your graves. I will put My Spirit in you, and you shall live, and I will place you in your own land. Then you shall know that I, the LORD, have spoken it and performed it," says the LORD.

Ezekiel 39:29

And I will not hide My face from them anymore; for I shall have poured out My Spirit on the house of Israel,' says the Lord GOD.

Joel 2:28-32

And it shall come to pass afterward That I will pour out My Spirit on all flesh; Your sons and your daughters shall prophesy, Your old men shall dream dreams, Your young men shall see visions. And also on My menservants and on My maidservants I will pour out My Spirit in those days. "And I will show wonders in the heavens and in the earth: Blood and fire and pillars of smoke. The sun shall be turned into darkness, And the moon into blood, Before the coming of the great and awesome day of the LORD. And it shall come to pass That whoever calls on the name of the LORD Shall be saved. For in Mount Zion and in Jerusalem there shall be deliverance, As the LORD has said, Among the remnant whom the LORD calls."

Acts 2:14-16

But Peter, standing up with the eleven, raised his voice and said to them, "Men of Judea and all who dwell in Jerusalem, let this be known to you, and heed my words. For these are not drunk, as you suppose, since it is only the third hour of the day. But this is what was spoken by the prophet Joel:"

Furthermore, did Jesus really mean He had to "depart" to send Himself back?

No New Testament text written twenty or more years later ever acknowledge this outpouring of the Spirit as a coming again of Jesus.

To the contrary, many subsequent, New Testament texts, again written after that event, were still anticipating this coming of Christ as yet future.

Besides, if what Jesus really meant was "the Holy Spirit would be with them always," why be so cryptic or mysterious? He wasn't cryptic anywhere else when He spoke about the Holy Spirit.

In John 14, for instance, Jesus spoke, distinctively and by name, about the Holy Spirit and the Holy Spirit's coming (see John 14:15-29).

"If you love Me, keep My commandments. And I will pray the Father, and He will give you another Helper, that He may abide with you forever—the Spirit of truth, whom the world cannot receive, because it neither sees Him nor knows Him; but you know Him, for He dwells with you and will be in you. I will not leave you orphans; I will come to you." "A little while longer and the world will see Me no more, but you will see Me. Because I live, you will live also. At that day you will know that I am in My Father, and you in Me, and I in you. He who has My commandments and keeps them, it is he who loves Me. And he who loves Me will be loved by My Father, and I will love him and manifest Myself to him." Judas (not Iscariot) said to Him, "Lord, how is it that You will manifest Yourself to us, and not to the world?" Jesus answered and said to him, "If anyone loves Me, he will keep My word; and My Father will love him, and We will come to him and make Our home with him. He who does not love Me does not keep My words; and the word which you hear is not Mine but the Father's who sent Me. "These things I have spoken to you while being present with you. But the Helper, the Holy Spirit, whom the Father will send in My name, He will teach you all things, and bring to your remembrance all things that I said to you. Peace I leave with you, My peace I give to you; not as the world gives do I give to you. Let not your heart be troubled, neither let it be afraid. You have heard Me say to you, 'I am going away and coming back to you.' If you loved Me, you would rejoice because I said, 'I am going to the Father,' for My Father is greater than I. "And now I have told you before it comes, that when it does come to pass, you may believe."

He clearly differentiated between Himself and the Holy Spirit by using the personal pronouns "I" and "him." Moreover, He spoke, clearly and plainly, in the rest of His Great Commission. So why not so in verse 20 as well?

I believe there is a much better explanation.

- That is, Jesus did speak, clearly, plainly, and distinctively.
- He meant exactly what He said.
- He, Jesus, the second Person of the Godhead, would both leave them to go to heaven and yet always be with them, and with us today as well, as opposed to the popular idea that He is currently absent from this present world and waiting to unscripturally return.

Most notably, when we compare different Bible translations with the original and literal Greek language, we find something quite interesting.

For instance, in the popular New International Version (NIV), the phrases "when he returns," "I will come back," "I am coming back," "going back," "until I return," and "Jesus … will come back" are found in only seven places in the New Testament, all of which is quoted from the NIV

Matthew 24:46

It will be good for that servant whose master finds him doing so when he returns.

Luke 12:43

It will be good for that servant whom the master finds doing so when he returns.

John 14:3

And if I go and prepare a place for you, I will come back and take you to be with me that you also may be where I am.

John 14:28

You heard me say, 'I am going away and I am coming back to you.' If you loved me, you would be glad that I am going to the Father, for the Father is greater than I."

John 16:28

I came from the Father and entered the world; now I am leaving the world and going back to the Father.

John 21:22-23

Jesus answered, "If I want him to remain alive until I return, what is that to you? You must follow me." Because of this, the rumour spread among the believers that this disciple would not die. But Jesus did not say that he would not die; he only said, "If I want him to remain alive until I return, what is that to you?"

Acts 1:11

"Men of Galilee," they said, "why do you stand here looking into the sky? This same Jesus, who has been taken from you into heaven, will come back in the same way you have seen him go into heaven."

The problem is, the words "return" and "back" are not in the original language. And the word "back," when added, unfortunately, conveys a nuance of being away and necessitating a "return." But Jesus never said He would "come back" or "return."

Correctly translated, His words are "cometh," "come again," "go to," "till I come," and just "come," respectively. The King James Version KJV translates these phrases correctly. Big difference!

COMPARATIVE

NIV	Literal Greek	KJV
(Incorrect Trans.)	(Original Text)	(Correct Trans.)
"when he returns" (Matthew 24:46)	"coming"	"cometh"
"when he returns" (Luke 12:43)	"coming"	"cometh"
"I will come back" (John 14:3)	"again I come"	"come again"
"I am coming back" (John 14:28)	"I... come"	"come again"
"going back" (John 16:28)	"go to"	"go to"
"until I return" (John 21:22-23)	"until I come"	"till I come"
"Jesus... will come back" (Acts 1:11)	"will come"	"shall so come"

Another revealing titbit comes from Jesus' unveiling in the Revelation's first chapter. Here, John (and we) see Jesus not off somewhere waiting to return someday, but instead, He's standing "among [in the midst] the lampstands" (Revelation 1:13, [KJV]).

Jesus explains that, "the seven lampstands are the seven churches" (Revelation 1:20b). This is more evidence that Jesus did not leave them but was with them, i.e., with the churches, in their midst.

Also notable, in my opinion, was the question Jesus' disciples asked Him the week before his crucifixion, "what will be the sign of your coming" (i.e., the Greek word translated as "coming" here is parousia and literally means "presence" as opposed to absence—Matthew 24:3).

They did not ask Him "what will be the sign of your return?" or "what will be the return of your presence?" Why not? It is because, in this context, His presence would remain with them and a return was not required.

It is my prayer that this chapter would have impacted you as it did me. Dr. John Noë has written extensively on many other subjects. For much more of his writings please see the information at the end of this book.

In our next chapter of this book the author would like to offer you his ponderings on Eschatology! We pray that as you read this chapter that you do so allow the Holy Spirit to guide you. Some of the truths presented will challenge some of your previous theology. As a matter you will be presented with the first four chapters of his book "Eschatology A Biblical View".

CHAPTER NINE
MY PONDERINGS ON ESCHATOLOGY

AS WE COMMENCE OUR JOURNEY IN SEEKING TO ARRIVE AT A CLEARER understanding of Eschatology (a branch of theology concerned with the final events in the history of the world or of humankind) I think it prudent we begin at the very beginning. From the Holy Scriptures we have recorded in it that God who existed all by Himself created the Heavens and the Earth and all that is in it. The obvious and valid question then is this—why creation? Allow me to leave that question for you to ponder as there is just no way for me to give you a valid reason as to why God created the Heavens and the Earth seeing that He existed perfectly all by Himself. However, you can certainly give it your best attempt...

However, let us seek to broach the whole issue of Eschatology from a sensible perspective. And as we do one of the things that we must understand is this—Audience Relevance is necessary for a proper biblical hermeneutic (Audience Relevance: What did the Scriptures meant to the audience it was written to at the time it was written?)

Another look at Acts 1:9-11

Now when He had spoken these things, while they watched, He was taken up, and a cloud received Him out of their sight. And while they looked steadfastly toward heaven as He went up, behold, two men stood by them in white apparel, who also said, "Men of Galilee, why do you stand gazing up into heaven? This same Jesus, who was taken up from you into heaven, will so come in like manner as you saw Him go into heaven."

When Scripture was written the prevailing thought then was that the world was FLAT! We now know that that was not true and the world is indeed round. So when it says that **ALL EYES** would see Jesus coming back to the Mt of Olives at that time it was easy to understand that from the perspective of the world being flat. But how do we interpret that Scripture in the light of the world being round and hanging in space, and up for everyone is different [people living in east, west, north, and south; up is entirely different...]? So from this perspective alone we could understand why many folks were wrong in their understanding of that particular text. And also know that Scripture was not being written on man's false understanding but on God's eternal view and on His understanding... Get it?

The question now becomes—was that Scripture written to a specific people in a specific time? It had to be! It is the only thing that seems to make sense!

What we need to get here is that the Scripture clearly states *"Men of Galilee, why do you stand gazing up into heaven?"* So this was clearly directed to the men of Galilee giving us the intended audience, who were all local people of the region of Galilee and not the entire world! The verse goes on to say *"This same Jesus, who was taken up from you into heaven, will so come in like manner as you saw Him go into heaven."* So the folks that were to see this same Jesus come back from Heaven where He ascended to, were the men of Galilee. That is as clear as day. This was not referring to a worldwide event!

As I continue my study on Eschatology there are two passages that are giving me an extremely hard time to fit into a clear and relevant context: Revelation 22:6-14

Then he said to me, "These words are faithful and true." And the Lord God of the holy prophets sent His angel to show His servants the things which must shortly take place. "Behold, I am coming quickly! Blessed is he who keeps the words of the prophecy of this book." Now I, John, saw and heard these things. And when I heard and saw, I fell down to worship before the feet of the angel who showed me these things. Then he said to me, "See that you do not do that. For I am your fellow servant, and of your brethren the prophets, and of those who keep the words of this book. Worship God." And he said to me, "Do not seal the words of the prophecy of this book, for the time is at hand. He who is unjust, let him be unjust still; he who is filthy, let him be filthy still; he who is righteous, let him be righteous still; he who is holy, let him be holy still." "And behold, I am coming quickly, and My reward is with Me, to give to every one according to his work. I am the Alpha and the Omega, the Beginning and the End, the First and the Last." Blessed are those who do His commandments, that they may have the right to the tree of life, and may enter through the gates into the city.

1 Corinthians 15:22-30

For as in Adam all die, even so in Christ all shall be made alive. But each one in his own order: Christ the firstfruits, afterward those who are Christ's at His coming. Then comes the end, when He delivers the kingdom to God the Father, when He puts an end to all rule and all authority and power. For He must reign till He has put all enemies under His feet. The last enemy that will be destroyed is death. For "He has put all things under His feet." But when He says "all things are put under Him," it is evident that He who put all things under Him is excepted. Now when all things are made subject to Him, then the Son Himself will also be subject to Him who put all things under Him, that God may be all in all. Otherwise, what will they do who are baptized for the dead, if the dead do not rise at all? Why then are they baptized for the dead? And why do we stand in jeopardy every hour?

So far many passages point to the idea that Jesus Christ returned to the earth in the Early Church but there are still some that point to another coming and the two above seem to lend validity to such thinking...

Revelation 22:6-14... key verse is verse 10...

Then he told me, "Do not seal up the words of the prophecy of this book, because the time is near.

The angel told John to not seal of the words of the book, because the time is near....

Now, look at this in contrast to what the angel of the Lord shares with Daniel about the book in Daniel 12:9

He replied, "Go your way, Daniel, because the words are closed up and sealed until the time of the end. 10 Many will be purified, made spotless and refined, but the wicked will continue to be wicked. None of the wicked will understand, but those who are wise will understand.

Both John and Daniel are hearing information pertaining to the 'end'... Daniel is told to seal up the words... John is told to not seal up the words... because the time that Daniel had seen was near...

For 1 Corinthians 15:22-30, in the entire 15th chapter, Paul is reassuring the people about Christ's resurrection, and their resurrection to come...

Verse 1 *Now, brothers, I want to remind you of the gospel I preached to you, which you received and on which you have taken your stand...*

He proceeds to talk about the eyewitness accounts in verses 3-7...

For I delivered to you first of all that which I also received: that Christ died for our sins according to the Scriptures, and that He was buried, and that He rose again the third day according to the Scriptures, and that He was seen by Cephas, then by the twelve. After that He was seen by over five hundred brethren at once, of whom the greater part remain to the present, but some have fallen asleep. After that He was seen by James, then by all the apostles.

Then he addresses those that didn't believe in the resurrection in verses 12-18...

Now if Christ is preached that He has been raised from the dead, how do some among you say that there is no resurrection of the dead? But if there is no resurrection of the dead, then Christ is not risen. And if Christ is not risen, then our preaching is empty and your faith is also empty. Yes, and we are found false witnesses of God, because we have testified of God that He raised up Christ, whom He did not raise up—if in fact the dead do not rise. For if the dead do not rise, then Christ is not risen. And if Christ is not risen, your faith is futile; you are still in your sins! Then also those who have fallen asleep in Christ have perished.

In verse 34, Paul exhorts them to come back to their senses, regarding the truth of the resurrection...

Awake to righteousness, and do not sin; for some do not have the knowledge of God. I speak this to your shame.

Verse 23 (*But each one in his own order: Christ the firstfruits, afterward those who are Christ's at His coming.*) is constrained to the audience (Corinthian church), but the principle applies eternally...

"The end" spoken of in verse 24 is only in reference to the closing of the Judaic theocratic system/kingdom. The Old Covenant Law was going to end and that is what Paul was speaking to here...

Then comes the end, when He delivers the kingdom to God the Father, when He puts an end to all rule and all authority and power.

This was the sign of the New Thing... those that are in Christ are freed from the clutches of death, which is the last enemy... the enemy that can keep one separated (in outer darkness) from God...

But Jesus is the Way, the Truth, and the Life!!!

2 Timothy 1:10

but it has now been revealed through the appearing of our Saviour, Christ Jesus, who has destroyed death and has brought life and immortality to light through the gospel.

John 8:51

I tell you the truth, if anyone keeps my word, he will never see death.

John 11:26

and whoever lives and believes in me will never die. Do you believe this?

...and of course...
John 3:16

For God so loved the world that he gave his one and only Son, that whoever believes in him shall not perish but have eternal life.

So, the prerequisite is to believe in Jesus and keeping His words!
Okay so do you see the possibility of another coming of Jesus? When the dead in Christ would rise? We would answer this in our next chapter!

Chapter Ten
My Ponderings on Jesus The First Fruit Of The Dead

To answer the question do you see the possibility of "**another**" revealing/ coming of Jesus, when the dead in Christ would rise? The answer would have to be a resounding No! And here is why: He was the First Fruit... so when He came in circa 70AD, everyone from that point on, into eternity, are part of the "*those who belong to him*", in 1 Corinthians 15:23...

Ok, I know some might be saying that this is not enough to prove my point, so allow me some time here to further explain this to you, from an article that I have found to be very well written and researched. This article is researched from the following link:[1]

Today some might wonder, why so much angst over the Messiah? After all, we have managed thus far without him. Do we really need a Messiah? Perhaps the longing seems to express a childlike hope in a hero on whom most of our people have long since given up. For many, the Messiah seems like little more than an ancient Jewish version of Santa or Superman. But don't miss the deeper emotion this "sorely perplexed" young rabbi felt. His cold fear was simply stated in the sentence, "Can it be the coming of the Messiah has passed and the promise has not been fulfilled?"

---

[1] https://jewsforjesus.org/publications/issues/issues-v13-n02/four-startling-facts-about-the-identity-of-the-messiah/

What else would drive the young man to push past his fears of the curse the rabbis had laid upon whomever would dare to calculate the timing of such things? Perhaps a greater fear of not knowing, of always wondering if God had made a promise—and broken it. For if the Holy Writings indeed predicted that the Anointed One would come within certain time parameters, and if he had not come, what other conclusion could one reach? A Messiah who never comes is maybe not such a big deal. But a God who spells out his promises in great detail and is then framed by those very details as a promise-breaker, is frightening, if not tragic, whether or not a person is religious.

The God who is described in the Jewish Bible is by definition all-knowing, all-powerful, just, good and deserving of trust. But what if God is not all these things? What if God is real but a liar and a fraud? It would take a brave person to explore such a shocking possibility. And that is exactly what Rabbi Leopold Cohn was willing to do more than 100 years ago.

Cohn was not the only one who realized the implications of a prophecy as exact as Daniel 9. Another young Jew, Rachmiel Frydland, grappled with the meaning of the passage and the ramifications of the timetable. Frydland, well versed in Talmud and Mishnah, also recognized that it would take some courage to study it:

The Jewish people rarely study the Book of Daniel because many rabbinic Jews were misled attempting to interpret Daniel's cryptic "times." Some were led so far astray that they came to believe in false messiahs, and therefore Talmudic Jews frowned on students who studied Daniel with a view of finding out the time of the Messiah. However, religious Jews knew that this book revealed more about Messiah than any other book.[2]

Frydland, like Cohn, overcame his fears and uncertainties and looked into the interpretation of this mysterious passage. What did the two men discover?

Fact One: the Messiah's appearance was locked into a fixed time.

Fact Two: that fixed time was while the Second Temple was still standing.

Fact Three: the Messiah had to come from a specific lineage that was only verifiable through the Temple records.

---

[2] Rachmiel Frydland, *When Being Jewish Was a Crime* (Nashville: Thomas Nelson Pub., 1978) p.72.

And the **fourth startling fact** is that the Messiah had to die a violent death. The details of these facts together present some of the strongest evidence that He has in fact already come.

FACT ONE: THE MESSIAH'S APPEARANCE WAS LOCKED INTO A FIXED TIME.

Ever hear the parental refrain, "You'll get your answer when the Messiah comes"? And to the response, "When will the Messiah come, Dad?" the answer is, "Who knows?"

But we **can** know the answer, in detail. It is in the book of Daniel. This Prophet who lived during the time of our exile in Babylon received a vision that the Messiah would come 483 years after the command to restore Jerusalem and rebuild the Temple:

> *...that from the going forth of the command to restore and build Jerusalem until Messiah the Prince, there shall be seven weeks and sixty-two weeks; the street shall be built again, and the wall, even in troublesome times.* (Daniel 9:25)

The "clock" on these 69 "weeks" (units of seven years) began ticking when Artaxerxes issued a decree to Nehemiah to rebuild the Temple and restore the holy city of Jerusalem (see Nehemiah 2:1-8). While other decrees went forth, this was the only one that involved both the Temple and Jerusalem. History records this took place in Nisan (March/April) of 444 B.C.E. (see chart below). That would mean the Messiah would appear by 33 C.E. History does not record anyone, other than Yeshua (Jesus), who was from that time period and claimed to be the Messiah.[3]

FACT TWO: THE SECOND TEMPLE WOULD STILL BE STANDING WHEN MESSIAH CAME.

Daniel predicted that after the appearance of Messiah, *"...the people of the prince who is to come shall destroy the city and the sanctuary"* (verse 26). We know that occurred when Titus' Roman legions marched on Jerusalem in 70 C.E., destroying both the city and the Temple. The Talmud teaches that at that time people believed that the Messiah had already come. But

---

[3] Adapted from a chart prepared by Dr. Harold Hoehner for the book future HOPE by David Brickner, 1999.

His appearance was concealed from the Jews until they were rendered more worthy of His appearance.[4]

Other passages support the understanding that Messiah would come while the Temple was still standing. For example, the rabbis recognized that Psalm 118 would be sung to the Messiah when He arrived.[5]

Hoshienu—*Save now, I pray, O Lord; O Lord, I pray, send now prosperity. Blessed is he who comes in the name of the Lord! We have blessed you **from the house of the Lord*** [emphasis Author's]. (vv. 25,26)

The only way that they could bless the Messiah **from** the house of the Lord was if the Temple was still standing!

Haggai, who was in Jerusalem as the Second Temple was being built, made the messianic prediction that the *"glory of this last temple is to be greater than that of the first"* (2:9).[6] And Malachi confirmed it: *"Then suddenly the Lord you are seeking will come to his Temple; the messenger of the covenant, whom you desire, will come"* (3:1). Twelfth century Jewish scholar, Rabbi David Kimchi, referred to the Malachi verse, saying, "The Lord, the angel of the covenant, is the Messiah."[7]

According to Daniel, the Temple would not only be standing at Messiah's appearance, but it would then soon be destroyed. That Temple, the Second Temple, which was originally built by Ezra and beautified by Herod, was where Yeshua (Jesus) did most of his teaching and made startling claims for himself. The New Testament records the painful words of Jesus to those who spoke of how beautiful the Temple looked after its refurbishing under Herod: *"These things which you see—the days will come in which not one stone shall be left here upon another that shall not be thrown down."*[8] Was Jesus pointing to Daniel's prophecy being fulfilled? Less than 40 years later the destruction of the Temple was so thorough that, to this day, the exact location of the sanctuary is unknown.

---

[4] John Ankerberg, *The Case For Jesus The Messiah*, c.1989 Chattanooga, as cited in Franz Delitzsch and Paton Gloag, *The Messiahship of Christ*, Part Two, p.226.
[5] Risto Santala, *The Messiah in the Old Testament In Light of Rabbinical Writings* (Jerusalem: Keren Ahvah Meshihit, 1992), p.103.
[6] Haggai 2:6 is applied to the Messiah in Deb. R. 1 (ed. Warsh. P. 4b, line 15 from the top) according to Alfred Edersheim, *List of Old Testament Passages Messianically Applied in Rabbinic Writings* (Grand Rapids: Eerdmans, 1976) p.735.
[7] Santala, p.102,103.
[8] Luke 21:6

FACT THREE: THE MESSIAH'S LINEAGE COULD ONLY BE IDENTIFIABLE WHILE THE TEMPLE STOOD.

The coming of the Messiah had another time constraint: it was connected to his descent from the tribe of Judah. Genesis 49:10, a well-recognized messianic prophecy,[9] indicated that Judah was to retain its identity until Shiloh (one of the names for the Messiah) was to come.

> *The scepter shall not depart from Judah, nor a lawgiver from between his feet,* **until Shiloh comes;** *[emphasis mine] and to Him shall be the obedience of the people.* (Genesis 49:10)

According to the book of Ezra (1:5-8), Judah's position was maintained throughout the 70 years' captivity in Babylon. It was also intact back in the Land, until the Romans made the kingdom of Judah a Roman province.[10] At that time the Sanhedrin was stripped of its authority and, according to Josephus, they [the members of the Sanhedrin] "covered their heads with ashes and their bodies with sackcloth, exclaiming, 'Woe unto us, for the sceptre has departed from Judah and the Messiah has not come.'"[11] While there was a provincial government in place, about 50 years later (in 70 c.e.) that too ended.

Not only was the Messiah to be from the lineage of Judah, but more specifically from the house of David: "*I have made a covenant with My chosen, I have sworn to My servant David: your seed I will establish forever, and build up your throne to all generations.*"[12] This messianic prophecy clearly refers to a descendent of David. Proof of such lineage was destroyed when the Temple was sacked. And while we do not have the Temple records, we do have the record of Yeshua's (Jesus') family tree in the accounts of His life by both Luke and Matthew. They both identify that He is from the house of David. We don't know anyone else who lived at that time and claimed to be the Messiah, who is descended from the tribe of Judah and the house of David, apart from Yeshua (Jesus).

FACT FOUR: THE MESSIAH WAS TO BE "CUT OFF."

The Daniel prophecy (v.26) says that after the seven weeks and sixty-two weeks, the Messiah would be cut off, but not for himself. This phrase "cut

---

[9] Ber. R. 98, ed. Warsh. P.174b; Sanhedrin 98b
[10] Josephus' *Antiquities* 17, chapter 13:1-5.
[11] Ibid.
12 Psalm 89:3-4

off" meant to be killed or die a violent death. Some of the Talmudic rabbis understood this: "In Daniel is delivered to us the end [the time of His appearance and death—Rabbi Jarchi] of the Messiah."[13]

The idea that the Messiah would die was not new to Judaism. Isaiah wrote of one who would suffer and die for the sins of the people: *"...For He was cut off from the land of the living; For the transgressions of My people He was stricken."*[14] Psalm 22 graphically portrays death by crucifixion, a method of execution not known to the psalmist writing 1000 years before Yeshua (Jesus) was crucified.

Could it have happened just as Daniel so carefully predicted? Counting 483 years after Artaxerxes' decree would bring us to 33 c.e. The Temple was destroyed in 70 c.e. That leaves a window of 37 years in which the Messiah from the tribe of Judah and the house of David could come. Not only that, but He was to die a violent death at that time. (End of quote from the article)

So then, there is no more waiting... now, to be absent from the body, is to be present with the Lord... we, are in fact, changed in a twinkling of any eye also... there's not a waiting period between our natural death and spiritual resurrection...

In essence, a 3rd coming would be contrary to this.

Paul was basically saying, during that time [2000 years ago], that there is coming a time, very soon, where we (they) will be raised up... he spoke about this because of the many that were becoming discouraged because they began to feel as if the Lord had abandoned them... thus, the constant encouraging to hold on and persevere...

Well that is my point exactly—Jesus rose from the dead ascended to Heaven and from what you are saying everyone that died from that time until He returned rose again from the dead when He came back. However, now that He came and went back to Heaven everyone that dies goes to be with Him. Some may ask: Why didn't they go to be with Him before and why did the dead have to rise and meet Him in the air then and never again? Absent from the body and to be present with the Lord should be true for everyone from the time that Jesus went back to Heaven...

All in God's timing... there was a set time/set number that had to come into the knowledge of God before His Parousia (coming)...

---

[13] Ibid. Ankerberg, p.226.
[14] Isaiah 53:8

Revelations 6:9-11

When He opened the fifth seal, I saw under the altar the souls of those who had been slain for the word of God and for the testimony which they held. And they cried with a loud voice, saying, "How long, O Lord, holy and true, until You judge and avenge our blood on those who dwell on the earth?" Then a white robe was given to each of them; and it was said to them that they should rest a little while longer, until both the number of their fellow servants and their brethren, who would be killed as they were, was completed.

We see here that there were a number of fellow servants/Believers that had to be killed to reach a certain "quota", or to fulfil something...

We also know from the gospels that Jesus told the disciples that He was going to prepare a place for them...

John 14:1-4

Let not your heart be troubled; you believe in God, believe also in Me. In My Father's house are many mansions; if it were not so, I would have told you. I go to prepare a place for you. And if I go and prepare a place for you, I will come again and receive you to Myself; that where I am, there you may be also. And where I go you know, and the way you know.

I believe the reason why Believers didn't go to be with Him before 70 AD was because He had to prepare a place for them...what ever that entails... I'm not going to pretend to know!

In regards to the dead rising, we are constrained to audience relevancy...

1 Corinthians 15, especially verses 51-52

Behold, I tell you a mystery: We shall not all sleep, but we shall all be changed—in a moment, in the twinkling of an eye, at the last trumpet. For the trumpet will sound, and the dead will be raised incorruptible, and we shall be changed.

1 Thessalonians 4, especially verses 15-18

For this we say to you by the word of the Lord, that we who are alive and remain until the coming of the Lord will by no means precede those who are asleep. For the Lord Himself will descend from heaven with a shout, with the voice of an archangel, and with the trumpet of God. And the dead in Christ will rise first. Then we who are alive and remain shall be caught up together with them in the clouds to meet the Lord in the air. And thus we shall always be with the Lord. Therefore comfort one another with these words.

We must keep in mind who Paul was speaking to, AND, Paul including himself in the resurrection equation... using the word "we" in both passages...

If the trumpets of these two passages are the same as the trumpets of the Olivet discourse, then we must keep this event (resurrection of the dead) in context.

But, we must also be able to distinguish the difference between historical events, and eternal principle. I believe this is where a lot of dispute and disagreement lies in some camps.

So, if someone asks the question now, "Is there a future resurrection?" I believe the answer is Yes, and No... Yes in that every Believer, after dying naturally, will be raised incorruptible... it's appointed to man once to die, then judgment... absent from the body, present with the Lord...

...But No, in regards to these passages referring to a future, literal Parousia... Scripture only speaks of one coming, where resurrection of the dead is associated with it...

Furthermore, when you study the principle of first fruits, you'll find that when the first is blessed, then the entire bundle, made after its kind, is blessed also. So in reference of the resurrection, Jesus, our First Fruit, was offered up to God (perhaps this is the reason for His leaving, and then returning...to offer Himself as the first fruit offering)... then those that believe in Him/follow Him/abide by-in His Word, they are blessed, as well as all that comes after them (us), because we are the bi-product of the seed(s) that was/were sewn... not only the Word, but also the Saints that planted and cultivated the Word throughout Church history.

Understood—the question remains why did we have the dead in Christ rise at His return and everyone else when they die going straight to be with the Lord... Why the difference seeing that both sets died after the burial, resurrection and ascension of Jesus Christ!!! The same thing that happens now when a Believer dies should have been the same thing for those who died between Jesus leaving earth and His return...

We are just going to have a discussion with Jesus and Paul when we see them! However, allow me to add my take on this. Again I am adding my take and NOT a biblical interpretation. I believe that this was so because of the crossover period between the death, burial and resurrection of Jesus and the complete, physical destruction of the Temple and Jerusalem circa AD 70.

Again remember that there was one generation that lived when the Temple still stood and the sacrifices were still being practiced according to the Old Covenant and the 1st Century Apostles who were being given the words and revelation of the New Testament or Covenant. However, once that Temple was destroyed to the fulfilment of the words spoken by Jesus and that initial resurrection took place then everyone who died in the Lord thereafter immediately faced judgement and was also immediately translated into the Presence of the Lord.

But I think the safest thing to do is keep Scripture in context... there's just no reference to a future resurrection of the dead... to assume so would then be adding to the letter...

Revelations 22:18-19

For I testify to everyone who hears the words of the prophecy of this book: If anyone adds to these things, God will add to him the plagues that are written in this book; and if anyone takes away from the words of the book of this prophecy, God shall take away his part from the Book of Life, from the holy city, and from the things which are written in this book.

This is why correct eschatology is such a serious thing... futurists/dispensationalists are adding to what is confined in Scripture... the amazing thing is there are many that understand what happened in 70 AD, but still believe in a future coming... which would then be a 3rd and 4th coming! Absolutely non-scriptural!!... A 3rd coming being a future rapture... then a 4th being a "descending New Jerusalem"...

Absolutely wrong...it's nothing short of fantasy, disillusionment, and escapism.

I think you are missing my point and the question that I am asking... Something is inconsistent and from what you are saying is that there was a resurrection of the dead [of Born-Again, Spirit-Filled Believers] after Jesus went to Heaven and returned; but for some reason that has since stopped without any valid reason or explanation... That is what I need to know—WHY did that happen? I never spoke about any future rapture, as I do not believe in that... However, something is missing that needs explaining and I would get it, eventually...

I understand what you're asking... why is there a difference in the manner of resurrections, then and now. I cannot answer that question, but with what has been written in Scripture. The one thing that we do know is that until that time (70 AD), those who died "remained in their lot" until the "end of days". Because this was told to Daniel in Daniel 12:13, I believe that this has to include the righteous and faithful before Christ, and those that believed in Jesus during His earthly ministry and afterward, all the way up to 70 AD. So this is the major difference between then and now.

UNDERSTANDING THE LAW AS IT RELATES TO THE RESURRECTION:

1 Corinthians 15:56 (*The sting of death is sin, and the strength of sin is the law.*) put the entire chapter in context with the passing of the law. The law passed in 70 A.D with the destruction of the Temple.

I believe that the law was fulfilled when Jesus Christ became The Perfect Sacrifice—The Lamb of God who died for the sins of the world [when He declared that it was finished on the Cross—I believe at that point it was indeed finished; the law included]. The destruction of the Temple was as a result of that!

To suggest that the law passed in 70AD is to suggest that two systems were working and valid between the ascension of Jesus and His return, and we know that that is not true. Yes, the two systems were working, but only One was valid as John the Baptist bridged the gap between the Old and New Testaments and Jesus fulfilled all the requirements of the law and then established the new way through His death and resurrection. Fifty days after His ascension the Holy Spirit arrived and thousands of

Jews [followers of the OT law] were saved. Some of them because of their unbelief and hardness of heart continued to worship under the OT law until God decided enough was enough and destroyed the Temple...

In the following section the author would like to share a bit on his ponderings of the "End Times"!

CHAPTER ELEVEN
MY PONDERINGS ON UNDERSTANDING THE END TIMES

BEFORE MOVING FORWARD LET ME SAY THIS—DO NOT GET YOURSELF IN A HISSY FIT as we continue. We need to know that we are in a path of PROGRESSIVE REVELATION AND UNDERSTANDING. Also note that your understanding of this will not impact on your bring SAVED... You are SAVED and once you maintain your walk with God you will be fine. However, how we understand what the Scripture speaks regarding *the end times* will certainly help in our confidence with our walk with God. And we must be the type of Saints that understand that we know in part, but maintain our quest for that which is perfect... So here we go!!

And again, this book is being written from a TEACHING ANOINTING and PERSPECTIVE and not a preaching/impartational anointing. So again, while this may not be your style I would recommend that you make the shift and stick with this study [deeply looking into the Word of God] as it could possibly change your life!

We are looking at what the Scriptures really have to say concerning the "*last days*" as we seek to have an accurate Understanding... There is just so much error and false prophecies concerning the "*last days*" and the *end* of all things going around that we need to have a correct understanding of this...

For example: Recently we had the Mayan calendar interpreted: those who interpreted it, saying that the world would have ended in December

2012... Some took a bit more "precaution" and said that there was a window between September 2011 and September 2013 for the world to end... We knew before the dates came and went that they were both false.

And yet with all the false prophecies that have gone [and we are only speaking about those in our lifetime – not to mention the untold numbers of those that went in the hundreds or even thousands of years before us] and the many more that will come most Christians are not studying the Scriptures to come to a sensible and accurate understanding of the "end-times"... We are seeking to do just that!!!

Many Believers are still not taking the time to explore God's Word for truth about the **end times** for themselves... And many Leaders who have studied the Word has done so with prejudiced lens not using EXEGESIS (critical explanation of a text of Scripture)—letting Scripture interpret Scripture...

The Italians have a saying, "**traduttore, traditore**." It literally means, "**translator, traitor**." Or more freely, "**all translators are traitors**."

So as one study the Word of God there is much need to check and double check original words that if translated wrongly could give an inaccurate understanding of what was originally stated.

As we go into this study here are a few things that I would like for us to fully understand:

1.   The Bible is a Book outlining Two Covenants for God's dealing with mankind!

2.   The Old Covenant or Testament was written explicitly to the Jews (God's Chosen People at the time)...

3.   The New Testament was written to the Jews to signal the END to the Old Covenant and the establishment of the NEW!

4.   The New Testament was also written to the 1st Century Believers as to how the New Nation called THE CHURCH should live in relation to Almighty God!!!

5.   That the Scripture in it's original content had no Chapters and Verses and were placed there by the translators of the original manuscripts.

6.   That the Old Testament completely and totally came to an end around 70AD and was replaced by a New Covenant (The New Testament), which is referred to as an Everlasting Covenant.

7. That there is no reference whatsoever pointing to another Covenant to come!

So as we proceed please note that for our study I would be using some material from Harold Eberle of Worldcast Ministries in Yakima WA State and co-author of the book "Victorious Eschatology", which can be purchased online at Amazon. So let's launch deeper into this study... Used by permission...

One of the most amazing studies of the Covenants is the study of the Eschatology of the Covenants.

The word "Eschatology" means: "Any system of doctrines concerning last, or final, matters". The word comes from the Greek word "E*schato*", meaning: "*last*". *So it is the study of those things, which are to occur last, the things that comes at the end of the Covenant. We are introduced to these "last" events over and over in the Old Testament with the phrases "Last Days", and "Latter Days". Here are a few of them.*

> *"And Jacob called unto his sons, and said, Gather yourselves together, that I may tell you that which shall befall you in THE LAST DAYS."* Genesis 49:1

> *"And now, behold, I go unto my people: come therefore, and I will advertise thee what this people shall do to thy people in THE LATTER DAYS."* Numbers 24:14

> *"When thou art in tribulation, and all these things are come upon thee, even in THE LATTER DAYS, if thou turn to the LORD thy God, and shalt be obedient unto his voice;"* Deuteronomy 4:30

> *"For I know that after my death ye will utterly corrupt yourselves, and turn aside from the way which I have commanded you; and evil will befall you in THE LATTER DAYS; because ye will do evil in the sight of the LORD, to provoke him to anger through the work of your hands."* Deuteronomy 31:29

> *"And it shall come to pass in THE LAST DAYS, that the mountain of the LORD's house shall be established in the top of the mountains,*

and shall be exalted above the hills; and all nations shall flow unto it." Isaiah 2:2

"And it shall come to pass in THE LAST DAYS, that the mountain of the LORD's house shall be established in the top of the mountains, and shall be exalted above the hills; and all nations shall flow unto it." Daniel 2:48

"Now I am come to make thee understand what shall befall thy people in THE LATTER DAYS: for yet the vision is for many days." Daniel 10:14

If you go back to each text and look at the surrounding passages you will find that there is no doubt that each one of these refers to the **Last Days Of Israel And Their Covenant**. So when we come to the New Testament and we begin to find these same phrases used; what should we conclude?

"And it shall come to pass in THE LAST DAYS, saith God, I will pour out of my Spirit upon all flesh: and your sons and your daughters shall prophesy, and your young men shall see visions, and your old men shall dream dreams:" Acts 2:17

This know also, that in THE LAST DAYS perilous times shall come." 2 Timothy 3:1

"Hath in THESE LAST DAYS spoken unto us by his Son, whom he hath appointed heir of all things, by whom also he made the worlds;" Hebrews 1:2

"Your gold and silver is cankered; and the rust of them shall be a witness against you, and shall eat your flesh as it were fire. Ye have heaped treasure together for THE LAST DAYS." James 5:3

"Knowing this first, that there shall come in THE LAST DAYS scoffers, walking after their own lusts," 2 Peter 3:3

"Little children, it is the LAST TIME: and as ye have heard that antichrist shall come, even now are there many antichrists; whereby we know that it is the LAST TIME." 1 John 2:18

COVENANT DURATION:

Can we conclude that since the Old Testament writers were writing to a Hebrew audience and about the Nation of Israel that when we come to the New Testament, that the Apostles who were ALL Jewish and members of the Nation of Israel, ministering to a predominant Jewish audience would actually change the meaning and application of the terms? I do not think that is a plausible possibility.

- If they were to change the meaning and application of the term Last Days, then where did they announce such a change?
- If they did not announce or indicate a paradigm shift in this area then why would we assume that we could insert our meaning to the phrase rather than their first century inspired meaning?

COVENANT DURATION:

Question: When did the Old Covenant come to an end?

Answer: When Jesus died on the Cross, and His Blood was spilled to ratify this New Covenant.

However, there was still a transition period between that time and when the Symbols of the Old were completely destroyed and the establishment of the New came fully into effect.

The strength of the Old covenant was in the physical Temple and it's rituals. So it was absolutely important that these symbols were completely removed...

Covenant Duration is another vital reason why these phrases (end-times, last-days, last-times, latter-days, etc) used to describe Israel's "last days in the Old Testament" should be continued to be applied to Israel's last days in the New Testament. Apostle Paul writes: 2 Corinthians 3:7

But if the ministration of death, written and engraven in stones, was glorious, so that the children of Israel could not stedfastly behold the face of Moses for the glory of his countenance; which glory was to be done away:

- Paul describes the Old Covenant as a "ministration of death", "Engraven in Stone"
- He then goes on to declare that it " -- was to be done away (with)" The Old Covenant had an end.
- This end is one of the most documented and recognized ends to a countries history and existence in all of recorded history. The destruction of the Jewish Temple in 70 AD is disputed by very few as the end of the Old Covenant of Israel with God.
- Paul compares this passing Old Covenant with the New Covenant, which he says is going to remain.

For if that which is done away was glorious, much more that which remaineth is glorious. 2 Corinthians 3:11

All through the Old Testaments, Moses and the Prophets wrote about the "Last Days" or "Latter Days" of that Old Covenant. They also prophesied that there would come a New Covenant.

"Behold, the days come, saith the LORD, that I will make a new covenant with the house of Israel, and with the house of Judah: Not according to the covenant that I made with their fathers in the day that I took them by the hand to bring them out of the land of Egypt; which my covenant they brake, although I was an husband unto them, saith the LORD:" Jeremiah 31:31-32

Other Prophets wrote about this New Covenant as well. They all agreed that this New Covenant would be an **Eternal or "Everlasting" Covenant.**

CHAPTER TWELVE
MY PONDERINGS ON UNDERSTANDING
THE NEW COVENANT

PROPHECIES ABOUT THE NEW COVENANT:

Incline your ear, and come unto me: hear, and your soul shall live; and I will make an everlasting covenant with you, even the sure mercies of David. Isaiah 55:3

For I the LORD love judgment, I hate robbery for burnt offering; and I will direct their work in truth, and I will make an everlasting covenant with them. Isaiah 61:8

And I will make an everlasting covenant with them, that I will not turn away from them, to do them good; but I will put my fear in their hearts, that they shall not depart from me. Jeremiah 32:40

Moreover I will make a covenant of peace with them; it shall be an everlasting covenant with them: and I will place them, and multiply them, and will set my sanctuary in the midst of them for evermore. Ezekiel 37:26

But now hath he obtained a more excellent ministry, by how much also he is the mediator of a better covenant, which was established upon better promises. Hebrews 8:6

In that he saith, A new covenant, he hath made the first old. Now that which decayeth and waxeth old is ready to vanish away. Hebrews 8:13

Now the God of peace, that brought again from the dead our Lord Jesus, that great shepherd of the sheep, through the blood of the everlasting covenant, Hebrews 13:20

NEW COVENANT DURATION:

- In reading these passages from Hebrews we see that the author is confirming to his Jewish (Hebrew) audience that the New Covenant is "better" and established upon "Better promises".
- The Author of the Book of Hebrews re-affirms that the Old Covenant was vanishing away, meaning it had an end.
- And then he agrees with the Prophets of the Old Testament that the New Covenant established through the Blood of Jesus Christ is an "**Everlasting Covenant**".

Let Us Consider For A Moment The Nature Of This New (Eternal) Covenant:

- In contrast to the Old Covenant it is built on better promises,
- It is a Covenant of life and not death,
- And it has no end.
- So it can be said that this New Covenant has no "Last Days".
- By definition a thing with no end would never have any last day or last days.
- So again the New Testament writers had to be writing about the end of the Old Covenant when they used the phrase "Last Days".

In addition, remember the definition of the term "Eschatology"—the study of last things. If this were the case, then how can we impose an Eschatology on a Covenant that has "No End"?

- Can the New Covenant, which has no end, actually have an Eschatology? But definition it cannot.

Paul Even Confirms This Never-Ending Nature Of The New Covenant When He Writes: Ephesians 3:21

Unto him be glory in the church by Christ Jesus throughout all ages, world without end. Amen. KJV

To Him be glory in the church and in Christ Jesus throughout all generations forever and ever. Amen (so be it). AMP

Unto him be glory in the assembly (church) in Christ Jesus to all the generations of the age of the ages. Amen. YLT

Okay so now that we have dealt with the whole issue of the Covenants and to some extent what the Bible meant when it referred to "The Last Days" here is what I am hoping we would cover in this series:

- In this series I am hoping that we would get through the Prophecies recorded in Matthew 24.
- We will discuss some issues that are key in considering that a lot of the Prophecies in the Bible have already been fulfilled.
- We will study the Prophecies in Chapters 2 and 9 of the Book of Daniel.
- We will hopefully work through the Book of Revelation.
- We will also delve into what the Scriptures actually say concerning the Jews the anti-Christ, and the rapture.
- Then we will seek to clarify what is meant by "the end-times" from a New Covenant perspective...

The more I looked at the widely accepted view that most if not all of the New Testament is yet to be fulfilled the more I realized that there were many Scriptures that simply do not fit into the scenario of events proposed by the futurists. After much in-depth study, over the years I have come to believe that the partial fulfilled view is more true to the Scriptures.

As we go through our study/teaching, we will revisit a few quotes from well-known Preachers, Teachers, and Reformers that show how the Fathers of the Faith shared a victorious eschatology. Not every leader throughout Church history would explain every verse of the Bible the same way; however, the fundamental view that the Church will rise in victory and power before the return of Jesus Christ has been the predominant view of the Church for the past 2,000 years.

One thing in common with the Early Church Fathers was that they all believed in an Eschatology that was indeed Victorious—here is what some of the Early Church Fathers have said:

QUOTES – EARLY CHURCH FATHERS

Charles H. Spurgeon (1834-1892)
I myself believe that King Jesus will reign, and the idols be utterly abolished; but I expect the same power which turned the world upside down once, will still continue to do it. The Holy Ghost would never suffer the imputation to rest upon His holy name that He was not able to convert the world. (The Life and Work of Charles Haddon Spurgeon, 1992,4:2L0)

Jonathan Edwards (1703-1758)
The visible kingdom of Satan shall be overthrown, and the kingdom of Christ set up on the ruins of it, everywhere throughout the whole habitable globe. (The Works of Jonathan Edwards, L974, 488)

Origen of Alexandria (185-254)
It is evident that... every form of worship will be destroyed except the religion of Christ, which will alone prevail. And indeed it will one day triumph, as its principles take possession of the minds of men more and more every day. (Origen Against Celsus, 1660, 8:68) "Celsus was a pagan philosopher of his time!"

John Wesley (1703-1791)
All unprejudiced persons may see with their eyes, that He [God] is already renewing the face of the earth: And we have strong

reason to hope that the work he hath begun he will carry on unto the day of the Lord Jesus; that he will never intermit this blessed work of his Spirit until he has fulfilled all his promises, until he hath put a period to sin and misery, and infirmity, and death; and re-established universal holiness and happiness, and caused all the inhabitants of the earth to sing together "Hallelujah." (The Works of John Wesley)

In our next, and final chapter of this book the author would like to offer you his ponderings on GOLD!

Chapter Thirteen
My Ponderings On Gold

Remember life is a skill, and we need to acquire that skill so that we can be successful. This is not based on your level of education; the colour of your skin, where you live, nor whom you know—God can give you the skill to live life successful. Remember Daniel and his friends in Babylon, God gave them wisdom to live successfully even in their captivity! The greatest warfare to be won is the one within—Proverbs 25:28 states,

> *Whoever has no rule over his own spirit Is like a city broken down, without walls.*
> *A person without self-control is like a house with its doors and windows knocked out.* MSG

One of the ways that we can acquire the skills to be our utmost for the Lord is to allow Him to process our lives and refine us, as gold is refined. Here is what is said in the Book of Malachi: Malachi 3:2-3 says,

> *But who can endure the day of his coming? Who can stand when he appears? For he will be like a refiner's fire or a launderer's soap. He will sit as a refiner and purifier of silver; he will purify the Levites and refine them like gold and silver. Then the LORD will have men who will bring offerings in righteousness.*

So one of the things we see that Father want is for us to be purified and as such I would like for us to look at what it takes to have gold purified.

BUY GOLD, REFINED IN THE FIRE? YES!—REFINING GOLD

It is my understanding, that in ancient days the refiner would sit before the crucible, fixing his eye on the metal. He would do this to ensure that the heat was not too intense to destroy the metal, but that it remained in the fire at the right degree of heat, for the exact period of time.

The refiner knew exactly when the precious metal was ready, just as soon as he saw his own image reflected in the glowing mass. At that precise moment he knew the dross was completely removed, and his task was accomplished.

In like manner, our heavenly Refiner is sitting as our Purifier, waiting to see His Image reflected in us: Job 23:10 says,

But He knows the way that I take; When He has tested me, I shall come forth as gold.

Proverbs 17:3

The refining pot is for silver and the furnace for gold, But the LORD tests the hearts.

Isaiah 48:10

Behold, I have refined you, but not as silver; I have tested you in the furnace of affliction.

Hebrews 12:10-11

For they indeed for a few days chastened us as seemed best to them, but He for our profit, that we may be partakers of His holiness. Now no chastening seems to be joyful for the present, but painful; nevertheless, afterward it yields the peaceable fruit of righteousness to those who have been trained by it.

Have you been experiencing the Lord in this way? Have you been feeling the sense of a deep work being done in your heart? Rejoice, because the Refiner is at work, making you ready for the next and final phase so that He can shine through you to the utmost!

As soon as the raw gold has been refined, the Blacksmith takes it to the next stage. [15]Bang! The iron hammer of the smith is raised and brought down on the lump of freshly mined gold. Soon the gold begins to "*suffer*" many things at the smiths' hands. The gold, being very malleable, is squashed a bit, contorted, misshapen, and is soon hit again, and again, and again.

The gold is on an anvil, a hard place, where it is beaten torturously and in great agony until it takes on a shape it was not. It is pressed beyond endurance, beyond its limits, beyond its natural threshold of pain, until it is no longer recognizable as a lump, but only as gold. The very crystalline structure of the gold is changing and hardening. The Blacksmith continues to rain blow upon blow on the gold, hammering away, seemingly without mercy. The gold can only feel the pain, feel the unfairness of the circumstance, feel the sting of the hammer. The Blacksmith however, through eyes of faith, can see the thing of beauty and service that he is making, as he applies one crushing blow at a time.

Gold is a biblical symbol for God's nature. He says that the gold and silver are His Gold speaks of deity and silver speaks of redemption and salvation. The Bible, in many places, uses a peculiar phrase called "beaten gold."

Beaten gold was made by hammering it into very fine sheets, which were then folded over and beaten again and again until it reached the consistency required by the Blacksmith. The Blacksmith works, seeing the end from the beginning. With his eyes all he sees is a lump of gold before him, but with his mind he sees it being forged into a vessel of honour, fit for the Kings service.

The only gold used in the construction of [16]Moses' Tabernacle was beaten gold. When Solomon built the Temple and his own house, enormous amounts of gold were used. Please understand that it is only beaten gold that enters into divine service.

When we come to Christ, we are like a new lump of gold, mined from the mud pits of the world. We are born again and filled with His Spirit. We walk with God a bit, when suddenly trials and tribulations begin to hit

---

[15] Excerpt taken from and used by permission from a writing titled "Beaten Gold" by Bryan Huppert of www.SheepTrax.com

[16] Exodus chapters 36-37 read and see the extensive use of "beaten gold".

our lives. We begin to suffer losses and learn to live a new kind of life, a divine life where we are forged into the image of Jesus. We go through the fires of refinement, and just when we think it is all done, blow upon blow seem to hit us from every direction, and we wonder why this perceived judgment of God has come. Hebrews 10:31-36 says,

It is a fearful thing to fall into the hands of the living God. But recall the former days in which, after you were illuminated, you endured a great struggle with sufferings: partly while you were made a spectacle both by reproaches and tribulations, and partly while you became companions of those who were so treated; for you had compassion on me in my chains, and joyfully accepted the plundering of your goods, knowing that you have a better and an enduring possession for yourselves in heaven. Therefore do not cast away your confidence, which has great reward. For you have need of endurance, so that after you have done the will of God, you may receive the promise.

Hebrews 5:8

Though He was a Son, yet He learned obedience by the things which He suffered.

It is only through picking up our cross daily, and following the Lord, do we become beaten gold. Much is written on the refinement process, where gold is placed in the fire to be purified, and the dross removed. The Blacksmith knows that the gold is purified when he can see his reflection in it. The gold is now perfect and ready...for service? No! Ready for the anvil, the high place of sacrifice and death.

There are many cleaned up lumps of gold in the Kingdom of God, who will not submit to the hammer. They refuse to be transformed on the altar of the anvil. Thank God they are in the Kingdom, but they are of no practical use to the King. It is *only* after gold has been made pure that it can be first beaten into an unrecognizable shape, flattened out into a thin sheet, and then finally made into a vessel of honour. You cannot enter into your destiny in Christ until you have said, like Job—"Though he slay me, yet will I trust Him," (Job 13:15) and laid your life on the anvil, His will be done in you.

If we are to follow Jesus, we must daily take up our cross and follow Him to the Cross. It is through [17]many tribulations that we enter into the Kingdom of God. We must lay our lives as a living sacrifice upon the anvil of God's Altar, ready to die to our lumpy self and be hammered into the golden, glorious image of Jesus! Gold, the coveted king of metals must be hammered and humbled before the King of Creation.

It is one thing to desire to be used of God. It is quite another to be willing to die to self, and be forged finally into a useable vessel. The difference between being a beautiful little lump of gold and a golden vessel that can hold the King's new wine, is the willingness to die to self and willingly face the hammer and anvil.

The Word of God makes it very plain that there are different kinds of vessel in the Kingdom: 2 Timothy 2:19-21 says,

> *Nevertheless the solid foundation of God stands, having this seal: "The Lord knows those who are His," and, "Let everyone who names the name of Christ depart from iniquity." But in a great house there are not only vessels of gold and silver, but also of wood and clay, some for honour and some for dishonour. Therefore if anyone cleanses himself from the latter, he will be a vessel for honour, sanctified and useful for the Master, prepared for every good work.*

In Christ, we are precious gold in the eyes of God. Now the choice is ours, whether we want to be a beautiful, refined lump before His throne, or a finished vessel, fit for the Master's use? I know that I want to be a finished vessel, fit for the Master's use!

Mindsets have to do with a fixed attitude or habit of the mind or the prevailing attitude of the mind. Also it can refer to—*the dominant or regular belief, practice of the mind.* Albert Einstein said: ***"The significant problems we have cannot be solved at the same level of thinking we were at when we created them."*** And Apostle Paul declared "***...be made new in the attitude of your minds...***"—Ephesians 4:23! Are you experiencing changes in your mindsets?

The church that will thrive in the 21st Century will not be anchored to stale forms and programs, but will forge boldly into new territories, possessing them in the Name of the King, it will the church with the

---

[17] Acts 14:21-22

building mentality. One of the characteristics of this "new kind of church" is a people who will embrace the Scriptural **building model** rather than just the **blessing model. Jesus said the He would BUILD His Church! Blessings is a given!**

There is just so much more that could have be written however, I am going to stop here. It is my sincere pray that what is contained in this volume would be sufficient to take you to another level in the Lord. Be all that you can be for the Master, Jesus Christ our Lord!

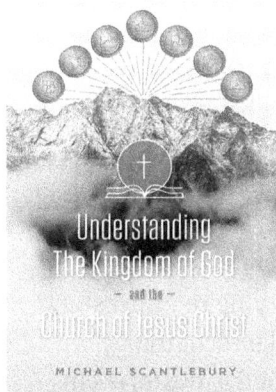

UNDERSTANDING THE KINGDOM OF GOD AND THE CHURCH OF JESUS CHRIST

"This book is a game changer and will teach you what it means to be part of This Kingdom."

Pastor Marilyn Bailey—Teleios Church, Johannesburg, South Africa

"There is perhaps no greater time to revisit the spiritual and practical understanding of the kingdom of God than right now.

Apostle Scantlebury addresses and corrects, common misconceptions, explains the contrasts in the Kingdom of God and the kingdom of darkness, properly aligns the Kingdom and the Church, and propels us toward a holistic understanding of Kingdom life in the earth.

With great patience and clear articulation, Apostle Scantlebury lays out a compelling case for the people of God to give priority to understanding and walking in the principles of the Kingdom of God in life and ministry.

Do yourself a favour; set aside some time to read through and study this transformative volume. You will be challenged, changed, and equipped to be a proper representative of the kingdom of God."

Apostle Eric L. Warren—Eric Warren Ministries
Charlotte, North Carolina, USA

ESCHATOLOGY – A BIBLICAL VIEW

If you were a time traveler and traveled back to the time of say Abraham Lincoln and told him you were from the future in 21st century. What if he asked you how people communicated in the 21st century, and now you had to try and explain say how an email works. How would you explain it?

Would you use something he would be familiar with to describe it? Perhaps you would tell him that in the future postmen would ride horses at 500 mile per hour. Or you might tell him you could deliver a message by train from New York to LA in less than one day. You're trying to find a way to communicate how "fast" an email really is. But you're trying to do in a way that wouldn't totally blow his mind.

That's kind of the conundrum we have when trying to understand difficult verses in the Bible, especially in themes like eschatology. The prophetic writers of Scripture had to convey God's mysteries in language that their readers would understand.

Fast forward now 2-3,000 years later, and we are reading these prophetic Scriptures through a 21st century lens, and sometimes coming up with all kinds of weird speculative interpretations because we didn't understand what those Scriptures would have meant to a first century believer, or a Jew living in the time of the OT prophets.

The book before you plan to delve deeper into this and much more as it seeks to present you with a sensible view of eschatology.

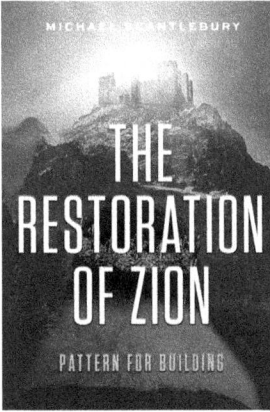

THE RESTORATION OF ZION

When you hear the word Zion, what comes to mind? As Christians, we've sung the choruses and the hymns about Zion or Mount Zion, but do we fully understand just what we're singing about? Do we know what it is? The Bible promises the full restoration of Zion, and if we don't fully know what Zion is, what then do we anticipate in terms of its restoration?

The greatest hindrance to accurate interpretation and application of Scripture is a futuristic view of Scripture. This futuristic view continues to rob the Believer of experiencing God in His fullness in the here and now.

In this book, we will uncover within the Scriptures exactly what Zion actually represents to the New Testament believer. So lay down any preconceived ideas you may have, delve into the pages of this book, and let it speak truth to you.

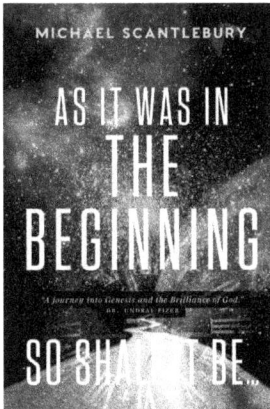

AS IT WAS IN THE BEGINNING SO SHALL IT BE...

Have you ever wondered about life and all of its intricacies? Why are we here on planet earth? What is out there in deep dark space? Who created it all in its majesty and wonder with the brilliancy of everything that surrounds us?

Since time began, man has tried to explain things regarding the known world. One forward thinker put forth a theory that the world was flat. That was refuted by more research. Study and research and pondering some more have revealed some truth about our world but not all the questions are yet answered.

While many of us as Christians enjoy documentaries on the pondering of the many ways we may have "gotten here" beginning with the theory of alien transports dropping us off, to the idea of a cosmic slime pit which one day came to life, so truly the only authority we have as born-again followers of Jesus Christ is the book of Genesis, the very first book of the Holy Scriptures, which simply states: "In the beginning God created the heavens and the earth." Genesis 1:1

We will broach the answers to these and other questions only God's inspired word, the Holy Bible will answer the many questions at hand.

We will begin our journey into the heart and mind of this incredible Creator to learn the reason and purpose for our existence. And as we take that incredible journey, we would seek to come to terms with the revealed, eventual outcome of our existence and life upon planet earth.

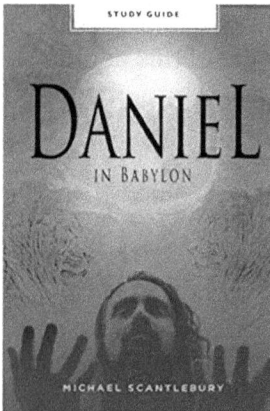

STUDY GUIDE – DANIEL IN BABYLON

This is an exciting study into the present truth lifestyle illustrated through the lives of Daniel and his friends. Whether you'll be meeting with others in a group or going through this book on your own, you've made an excellent decision by choosing to read **DANIEL in Babylon** and studying it in-depth with this guide.

This is a seminal study with strong Apostolic messaging, yet its flowing style allows for easy assimilation of biblical truths, and provides accurate insights for the cerebral believer, who like Daniel and his companions, are usually the target of the world system. In this book various methodologies are outlined through which, spiritual Babylon seeks to entice the brightest and best of every Godly generation, to acculturize, rob of spiritual identity and manipulate to promote world kingdom end.

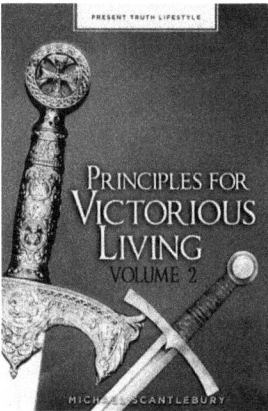

PRINCIPLES FOR VICTORIOUS LIVING VOLUME II

The initial purpose of the five-fold ministry is for the perfecting or maturing of the Saints, which leads to its next intention, which is the real work of the ministry of Jesus Christ, reconciling the world back to the Father. This book lends itself to help in the maturing of the Saints. It adds insight and strategies that help in achieving exponential personal growth preparing one for the real work of the ministry. This is a volume of information and revelation needed in such a time as this, when maturity and focus are the needed key components that bring us an overcoming victory in this realm and advance the Kingdom of God.

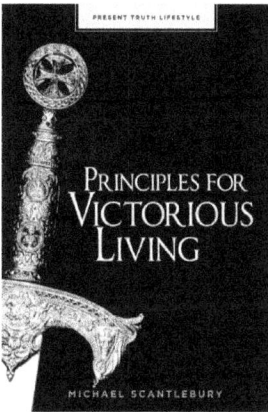

PRINCIPLES FOR VICTORIOUS LIVING VOL I

The information contained herein is well balanced with a spiritual maturity that keenly stems from wisdom and revelation in the knowledge of Christ. This is the anointing of an Apostle, and the truths that our brother shares will certainly cause you to excel in the Kingdom of God long before this life is over when later we enter the eternals. There's so much to experience today in this life, and Michael extracts so much from the Word of God to facilitate that. His insight of revelation and ability to interpret and articulate what his spirit receives from the Lord are powerful.

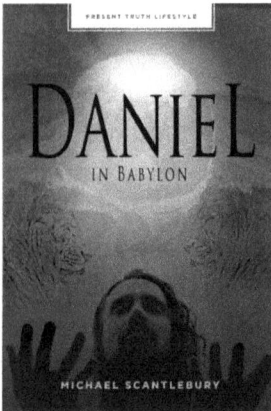

PRESENT TRUTH LIFESTYLE
– DANIEL IN BABYLON

This is a seminal study with strong Apostolic messaging, yet its flowing style allows for easy assimilation of biblical truths, and provides accurate insights for the cerebral believer, who like Daniel and his companions, are usually the target of the world system. In this book various methodologies are outlined through which, spiritual Babylon seeks to entice the brightest and best of every Godly generation, to acculturize, rob of spiritual identity and manipulate to promote world kingdom end.

But thanks be to God, there is still a generation in the earth spiritually alert enough to operate within the world system, yet deploy their talents and giftings to bring honour and glory to God. Those with the Daniel mindset will decode dreams and visions and interpret judgements written on the kingdoms of this world in this season.

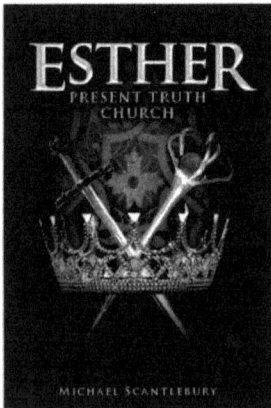

ESTHER PRESENT TRUTH CHURCH

In a season where the Church co-exists harmoniously with truth and error, this book provides us with a precision tool and well-calibrated instrument of change that is able to fine-tune the global Body of Christ.

The Book of Esther is rich with revelation that is still valid and applicable for the day in which we live. Hidden within its pages is a powerful "present truth" message. The lives of the people involved and the conditions that are seen have spiritual parallels for the Church. Our destiny as the Body of Christ is revealed. The preparations and conditions we must attain to are all similar.

THE FORTRESS CHURCH

According to Webster's English Dictionary "fortress" is defined as: a fortified place: stronghold, *especially*: A large and permanent fortification sometimes including a town. A place that is protected against attack. This book seeks to describe what is a "Fortress Church". We would be looking into the dynamics of this Church as described in Jacob's vision in Genesis Chapter 28, also as described by the Prophet Isaiah, in Isaiah Chapter 2 and as the one detailed in a Psalm of the sons of Korah in Psalms Chapter 48. We would also be looking at a working model of this type of church as found at Antioch in the Book of Acts. Finally we would be exploring The Church at Ephesus, where the Apostle Paul by the Holy Spirit revealed some powerful descriptions of The Church.

CALLED TO BE AN APOSTLE

This autobiography spans fifty-two years of my life on the earth thus far and I have the hope of living several more... Our home was always packed with young people and we did enjoy times of really wonderful fellowship! Although we were experiencing these wonderful times of fellowship my appetite and desire to grow in the things of God continued unabated. I continued to read anything and everything that I could put my hands on that would strengthen my life. I began reading Wigglesworth, Moody, Finney, Idahosa, Lake, and the list went on and on! But the more I read the more this question burned in my heart–"*why is it that every time we hear/read about a move of God, it is always miles away and in another country? Why can't I experience some of the things that I am reading about?*" Little did I know the Lord would answer that desire!

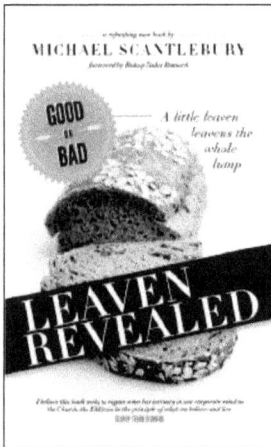

LEAVENED REVEALED

The Bible has a lot to say about *leaven* and its effects upon the Believer. Leaven as an ingredient gives a false sense of growth. In the New Testament there are at least six types of *leaven* spoken about and we will be exploring them in detail, in order to ensure that our lives are completely free of the first five, and completely influenced by the sixth! These types of leaven include the following: The leaven of the Pharisees; The leaven of the Sadducees; The leaven of the Galatians; The leaven of Herod; The leaven of the Corinthians. However, the Leaven of the Kingdom of God is the only type of leaven that has the power and capacity to bring about true growth and lasting change to our lives.

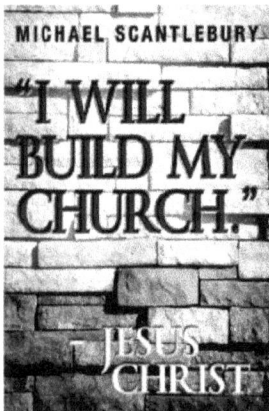

I WILL BUILD MY CHURCH — JESUS CHRIST

"For we are his *masterpiece*, created in Christ Jesus for good works that God prepared long ago to be our way of life." Ephesians 2:10

What a powerful picture of The Church of Jesus Christ–His Masterpiece! Reference to a *masterpiece* lends to the idea that there are other pieces and among them all, this particular one stands head and shoulders above the rest! This is so true when it comes to The Church that Jesus Christ is building; when you place it alongside everything else that God has created, The Church is by far His Masterpiece!

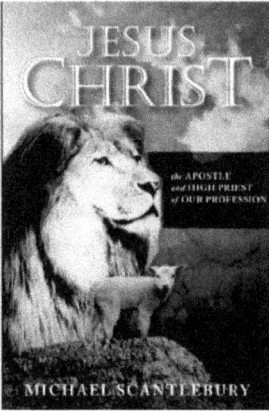

JESUS CHRIST THE APOSTLE AND HIGH PRIEST OF OUR PROFESSION

There is a dimension to the apostolic nature of Jesus Christ that I would like to capture in His one-on-one encounters with several people during the time He walked the face of the earth and functioned as Apostle. In this book we will explore several significant encounters that Jesus Christ had with different people where valuable principles and insight can be gleaned. They are designed to change your life.

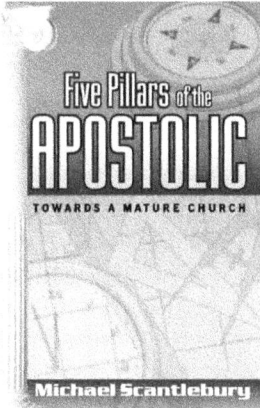

FIVE PILLARS OF THE APOSTOLIC

It has become very evident that a new day has dawned in the earth, as the Lord restores the foundational ministry of the Apostle back to His Church. This book will give you a clear and concise understanding of what the Holy Spirit is doing in The Church today.

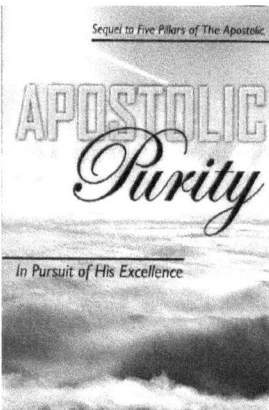

APOSTOLIC PURITY

In every dispensation, in every move of God's Holy Spirit to bring restoration and reformation to His Church, righteousness, holiness and purity has always been of utmost importance to the Lord. This book will challenge your to walk pure as you seek to fulfil God's Will for your life and ministry.

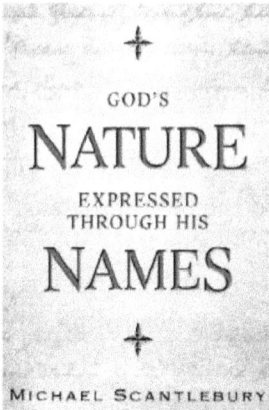

GOD'S NATURE EXPRESSED THROUGH HIS NAMES

How awesome it would be when we encounter God's Nature through the varied expressions of His Names. His Names give us reference and guidance as to how He works towards and in us as His people–and by extension to society! As a matter of fact it adds a whole new meaning to how you draw near to Him; and by this you can now begin to know His Ways because you have come into relationship with His Nature.

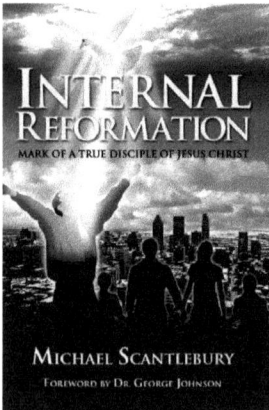

INTERNAL REFORMATION

Internal Reformation is multifaceted. It is an ecclesiology laying out the blue print of The Church Jesus Christ is building in today's world. At the same time it is a manual laying out the modus operandi of how Believers are called to function as dynamic, militant over-comers who are powerful because they carry internally the very character and DNA of Jesus Christ.

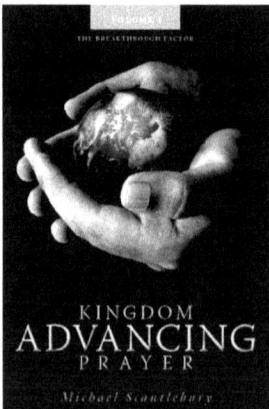

KINGDOM ADVANCING PRAYER VOLUME I

The Church of Jesus Christ is stronger and much more determined and equipped than she has ever been, and strong, aggressive, powerful, Spirit-Filled, Kingdom-centred prayers are being lifted in every nation in the earth. This kind of prayer is released from the heart of Father God into the hearts of His people, as we seek for His Glory to cover the earth as the waters cover the sea.

APOSTOLIC REFORMATION

If the axe is dull, And one does not sharpen the edge, Then he must use more strength; But wisdom brings success." (Ecclesiastes 10:10) For centuries The Church of Jesus Christ has been using quite a bit of strength while working with a dull axe (sword, Word of God, revelation), in trying to get the job done. This has been largely due to the fact that she has been functioning without Apostles, the ones who have been graced and anointed by the Lord, with the ability to sharpen.

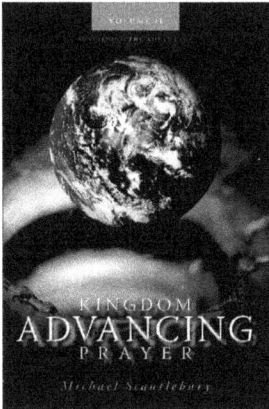

KINGDOM ADVANCING PRAYER VOLUME II

Prayer is calling for the Bridegroom's return, and for the Bride to be made ready. Prayers are storming the heavens and binding the "strong men" declaring and decreeing God's Kingdom rule in every jurisdiction. This is what we call Kingdom Advancing Prayer. What a *Glorious Day* to be *Alive* and to be in the *Will* and *Plan of Father God*! *Hallelujah*!

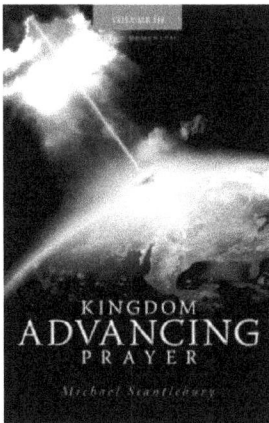

KINGDOM ADVANCING PRAYER VOLUME III

One of the keys to the amazing rise to greater functionality of The Church is the clear understanding of what we call Kingdom Advancing Prayer. This kind of prayer reaches into the very core of the demonic stronghold and destroys demonic kings and princes and establishes the Kingdom and Purpose of the Lord. This is the kind of prayer that Jesus Christ engaged in, to bring to pass the will of His Father while He was upon planet earth.

IDENTIFYING AND DEFEATING THE JEZEBEL SPIRIT

I declare to you with the greatest of conviction that we are living in the days when Malachi 4:5-6 is being fulfilled. Elijah in his day had to confront and deal with a false spiritual order and government that was established and set up by an evil woman called Jezebel and her spineless husband called Ahab. This spirit is still active in the earth and in The Church; however the Lord is restoring His holy Apostles and Prophets to identify and destroy this spirit as recorded in Revelation 2:18-23.

ADDITIONAL READING

Noe, John, Ph.D. *The Greater Jesus* (East2west Press, 2012).

www.ingramcontent.com/pod-product-compliance
Lightning Source LLC
Chambersburg PA
CBHW072012090426
42740CB00011B/2161